LONG-TERM CARE:

*Your Financial
Planning Guide*

LONG-TERM CARE:

*Your Financial
Planning Guide*

Phyllis Shelton

*Chris,
Thank for helping American
ur LT insurance!
Phyllis Shelton*

KENSINGTON BOOKS
http://www.kensingtonbooks.com

KENSINGTON BOOKS are published by

Kensington Publishing Corp.
850 Third Avenue
New York, NY 10022

All Kensington titles, imprints and distributed lines are available at special quantity discounts for bulk purchases for sales promotion, premiums, fund raising, educational or institutional use.

Special book excerpts or customized printings can also be created to fit specific needs.For details, write or phone the office of the Kensington Special Sales Manager: Kensington Publishing Corp., 850 Third Avenue, New York, NY, 10022. Attn. Special Sales Department. Phone: 1-800-221-2647.

Kensington and the K logo Reg. U.S. Pat. & TM Off.

ISBN 1-57566-641-3

First Kensington trade Paperback Printing: May, 2001
10 9 8 7 6 5 4 3 2 1

Printed in the United States of America

Table of Contents

INTRODUCTION

Christopher Reeve's tragic accident spotlighted a reality that many Americans have never faced. A long-term care need can hit at any time, at any age. At age 43, "Superman" fell into this huge category: 40% of people needing long-term care in this country are working-age adults, ages 18–64.[1]

Private health insurance doesn't cover long-term, chronic care for younger people and Medicare doesn't cover it for older people. Medicaid pays only if you spend most of your assets. So we have to take care of ourselves.

Are you a small business person, entrepreneur, or climbing the corporate ladder? If you are working 60+ hours per week as many of us do, and out of the blue, your spouse or parent or parent-in-law has an accident or stroke and needs long-term care, what will happen to your career? At an average of $50,000–$100,000 per year (depending on where you live) for daily home health care or nursing home care, most families don't know where to turn for help.

The American female today is projected to spend more years taking care of aging family members than her own children,[2] and by 2005, 37% of U.S. workers will be more concerned with caring for a parent than children.[3]

There's a solution, and a good one, for this dilemma, but it's not for everyone.

This book is dedicated to helping you determine if long-term care insurance is appropriate for you, your spouse and/or your parents. Since it is the fastest growing insurance product in the country, many people want information such as:

1. What are the chances for a government-funded program for long-term care? (see Chapter 1, *Prospects for Government Help*, p. 18.)

2. What are the tax advantages for long-term care insurance? (see Chapter 1, *Recent Health Care Reform*, p. 19.)

3. I've read several articles that advise me to wait until I'm 53 to buy long-term care insurance. Is this a good idea? (see Chapter 2, *The True Cost Of Waiting*, p. 65.)

4. I'm only 40. Wouldn't I be better off just saving the premium and paying for my own long-term care? (see Chapter 2, *Saving vs. LTC Insurance*, p. 67.)

As an insurance consultant and former LTC insurance agent, I am especially committed to providing current, meaningful information about long-term care insurance that is not available in any other publication. This book also will explain the other major programs that are impacted by the issue of long-term care, such as Medicare, Medicare supplement and the Medicaid (MediCal in California) benefit for long-term care, in addition to alternatives such as group LTC insurance, reverse mortgages, viatical and life settlements, life insurance/accelerated death policies, and in some states, a special Partnership program between private LTC insurance and Medicaid.

Please, let me caution you. This booklet is only a summary of the highlights of the various programs. It is not a legal description of benefits and should not be used as such. If you have questions about specific benefit features, you should consult an insurance agent you trust or your state's insurance department (See **Who to Call for Help**, p. 225), and any appropriate insurance policy contracts.

I hope you find this information helpful.

Phyllis Shelton
Nashville, Tennessee
May 2001

Chapter 1

Long-Term Care
and Your Financial Security

〜〜〜〜〜〜〜〜〜〜〜〜〜〜〜〜〜〜〜〜〜〜〜〜〜〜〜〜〜〜〜〜

"LTC will be THE burning health care issue of the 21st century, as baby boomers struggle to prepare for their own needs and take care of their parents as well. We must begin to prepare now for those challenges."

—Rep. Pete Stark (D-CA), upon introducing
The Omnibus Long-Term Care Act of 1999, August 1999

I was three when my grandparents moved in with us. My grandmother died unexpectedly two years later after gall bladder surgery. My grandfather was so sad. I still remember him crying after the funeral.

Born in 1886, my grandfather was blind, a diabetic who had to have a shot every day, and most importantly, my best friend. He listened with endless patience while I laboriously read the adventures of Nancy Drew, Cherry Ames, the Dana Girls, and Trixie Belden, none of which I ever finished. I think he also heard excerpts from Black Beauty and Beautiful Joe, my favorite animal books. Sometimes he returned the favor by telling me stories about his logging days in the East Tennessee mountains.

My mother was a nurse, worked nights while my father could be with us, and cared for my best friend almost ten years in our home, with my help of course. I didn't give him his daily insulin shot or plan his special diet or bathe him or dress him. But I gave him hours upon hours of my time, partially because I took the caregiving responsibility my mother assigned to me very seriously, but mostly because of how much I loved him. We had to be quiet while she slept, so I read him story upon story and fetched many glasses of water and led him to the bathroom when he asked me to. Sometimes I just crawled up on his lap to let him make whatever problem I encountered during the day go away. As I grew older, his room was my first stop when I got home from school.

My best friend went to a nursing home when I was 12. He never asked for help, but I knew my mother was struggling between giving him her best (he was incontinent by then) and caring for me and my three-year-old brother. She was also working double shifts at the hospital for extra money. We moved him to another nursing home once because she didn't think he was getting the best possible care. When he passed away two years later, I was devastated. My best friend was gone.

Twenty years later, my mother lost a two-year battle with cancer at age 54. I thought about my best friend and finally realized that what was a normal lifestyle for me as a child must have been a tremendous sacrifice for her.

Home and community-based care and nursing home care represent the largest out-of pocket expenses facing older Americans.[1]

Unfortunately, it is one of the only health care expenses that is not covered by group and individual health insurance, HMOs, retiree health plans or Medicare and Medicare supplements. This chapter presents information about why long-term care has become a national concern. Have you ever known anyone whose assets were totally destroyed by prolonged home health or nursing home care? A friend, a neighbor, a relative—or even you—could be one of the many, many Americans who face this plight each year.

The average annual cost nationally for nursing home care is about $57,000, or $157 per day for total costs, including semi-private room and board, drugs and medical supplies.[2] An eight-hour shift for a home health care aide through a home health agency is not far behind at about $128.[3] (In some parts of the country, the cost is an astronomical $320 per day, or over $116,000 per year, and home health care can easily cost $22+per hour.[4]) **These costs will at least triple in the next 20 years,** according to the U. S. General Accounting Office, June, 1991, with an average annual growth rate of 5.8%. (A similar projection is made for 1993-2008 by the Health Care Financing Administration.[5]) This means that the 50-year-old of today can expect to spend at least $310,000 (or over $600,000 in the highest cost areas) per year if he or she requires nursing home care at age 80. If both spouses need the care, the figure grows astronomically.

Do you find these projections hard to believe? The average semi-private nursing home cost in a 1990 Nashville, Tennessee cost survey was $60. That figure in the same survey published in January 2001 was $117—an average yearly growth rate of 6.25%.[6]

One out of four caregivers in a 1998 national home care survey reported providing care longer than five years.[7] The most recent national nursing home survey showed that although two-thirds of nursing home stays were three years or less, 14% of the patients stayed longer than five years.[8] Forty-seven percent of people over age 85 have some type of dementia, most commonly Alzheimer's[9] and an Alzheimer's patient can live an average of eight years and as many as 20 years.[10] A recent study showed that less than 2% of home health, nursing home and hospital bills with the primary diagnosis of Alzheimer's was reimbursed by private insurance or Medicare.[11]

Shaun Mabry, an independent insurance agent in Dallas, Georgia, knows these statistics firsthand. His grandmother spent 11 years in a nursing home with Alzheimer's until her death at age 83. His knowledge goes far beyond an extended duration of care, however. He also watched as his grandmother went from a "saintly, churchgoing person to a sailor"—Shaun's term for someone with very salty language and a totally unfamiliar, very unpleasant personality, a heartbreaking transition for Shaun's family.

This extremely high incidence of Alzheimer's coupled with 85+ being the fastest growing segment of the population make it easy to see why a national survey said that caregiving directly affects one out of four families in the United States, with just over 23% of all U.S. households containing at least one caregiver in the decade 1986–1996. Twenty-two percent of these caregivers provided care to two people and 8% to 3 or more![12]

Shaun Mabry's other grandmother provides an extreme example of multiple caregiving. At age 77, she is caring for her 78-year-old husband, Shaun's grandfather, who has

Alzheimer's, her 50-year-old daughter who had a stroke last year, and three grandchildren, all two-years-old, born two months apart. Her mother is still alive in Florida at age 106!

Combine this staggering volume of caregiving with a 1999 survey that reports that two-thirds of Americans say they could not afford to pay for more than two years of long-term care at $40,000 a year.[13] Given these statistics, it's no surprise that more than half of all nursing home residents run out of money within the first year and qualify for welfare (Medicaid).[14] As you can see, **long-term care is a family crisis for the year 2000 and beyond.**

The Odds Are 1 out of 2

While the general population perceives the risk of needing long-term care services to be less than 25%, the actual risk for needing long-term care (either home care or nursing home care) is **greater than 50%.**[15] For most of us, that won't be nursing home care, as most people will never be in a nursing home. But home care can cost just as much or more than being in a nursing home, depending on how much you have.

The increasing demand for long-term care is the result of several factors—the aging population, a shortage of caregivers in the home due to women working and children locating away from parents, and technology that prolongs life for victims of heart attacks, diabetes and the like, only to make it that much more likely the survivor will experience a stroke and need long-term care.[16] All these factors combine to make the need for long-term care escalate at a dizzying pace.

An Aging America

Consider this rapidly unfolding social phenomenon. In a little over 200 years, life expectancy has doubled in this nation. In frontier America only one in ten people could expect to see age 65, and today 10% of people over 65 have children over 65![17] Today, almost 80 percent of Americans will live past 65 and life expectancy is another 15 years for men and 19 years for women.[18] Currently, there are 35 million people over 65, some 13% of the population. By 2030, the number will grow to 70 million, or one-fifth of the population.[19] There are 72,000 Americans over the age of 100, and that number is expected to triple in 20 years.[20] And the real shocker? Based on projected trends, the Social Security Administration estimates that 12 million Americans alive today will bring in the NEXT century in 2100![21]

You may have heard of Jeanne Louise Calment of Arles, France, who lived longer than any human on record. She was 122 when she died August 5, 1997. She never lost her saucy personality, evidenced by a humorous anecdote from an interview she did at age 115. The reporter asked her how she saw the future, and she replied without hesitation, "Short, very short!" She was wrong, though, wasn't she? She still had another seven years to go![22]

One-third of all Americans (76 million people) were born between 1946 and 1964—a group we affectionately named the baby boomers. We are about to exchange that well-worn term for another. Instead of having a baby boom, we are on the verge of the country's first Senior Boom. One out of four people in the United States is already over 50. Movies and television over the last twenty years reflect this phenomena: *Space Cowboys, Grumpy Old Men I* and *II, Diagnosis Murder, Murder She Wrote, Matlock,* and the Oscar-award winning *Driving Miss Daisy.* Magazines like *Senior Golfer* and *Modern Maturity* enjoy readerships of millions. You can frequently see 50+ models like Lauren Hutton in fashion magazines and talent acts like Rod Stewart, The Rolling Stones and Tina Turner are still rocking audiences around the world.

In Akron, Ohio you can go to work for Mature Staffing Solutions, a successful employment agency specializing in workers in their 50's, 60's, 70's, and up to meet the community's demand for older workers. It's a win-win: Older workers tend to already have a pension and Medicare, so working part-time without benefits creates a low-maintenance, highly trained labor pool for grateful employers.[23]

February 15th is "Nathan Horner Day" in Greenville, Tennessee, in celebration of over 50 years of medical practice given to this small community by a beloved local physician whose waiting room still hosts at least 40 patients a week. Dr. Horner barely noticed his 82nd birthday.

We have managed to prolong life by overcoming a variety of contagious diseases, by utilizing sophisticated technology with heart, cancer and other catastrophic health conditions, and by taking better care of ourselves with diet and exercise, etc. While our great-grandparents would have been glad to have seen 60, Americans are now seeing ninth and even tenth decades. A survey from The Gerontological Society of America even suggests "the maximum individual longevity potential is over 130 years!"[24] Unfortunately, as one author put it, we may be buying ourselves a slow death, because long life doesn't guarantee long quality of life.[25] In reality, the longer we live, the greater the chance we will need long-term care. *And the people who take care of themselves the best will probably need long-term care the most, because they won't die suddenly of a massive heart attack or stroke— they'll just wear out slowly!*

All Ages Need Long-Term Care

Since long-term care is defined as care that simply takes care of people who are in chronic conditions with little or no progress, it can happen to people at any age. Few people realize that regular health insurance will not pay for a thirty-two-year-old who winds up in a coma with no progress after an automobile accident. A tragic example is "Superman" actor Christopher Reeve who is almost totally paralyzed after a horseback riding accident at age 43. After almost a decade of battling Parkinson's disease, thirty-eight-year-old actor Michael J. Fox announced his departure from his popular television series *Spin City* to spend time with his family and raise money to search for a cure. This adds him to the list of well-known victims of Parkinson's disease—a list that includes Muhammad Ali, former three-time world heavyweight champion, and U.S. Attorney General Janet Reno.

Forty-five-year-old Bob Dancey is paralyzed from the neck down after suffering the same spinal injury as actor Christopher Reeve, after getting knocked off his surf board by a wave and striking his head in shallow water. [26]

It's very important to realize that long-term care is not just an issue that affects older Americans. Over 40% of Americans receiving long-term care are *under* 65 years old.[27] Only ten percent of nursing home patients are in this younger age category[28]—the rest of the younger people are cared for in the community, mostly at home. Younger people need long-term care for automobile and sporting accidents, disabling events such as brain tumors, and disabling diseases such as muscular dystrophy, multiple sclerosis, Parkinson's and Lou Gehrig's disease. The federal government estimates up to 2 million Americans suffer some kind of traumatic brain injury each year—50,000 die, but 70,000 to 90,000 are disabled.[29] One-third of the 700,000 stroke victims in the United States each year are under 65![30]

At 52, Marla Everett* leads a simple life in a one bedroom Airstream trailer on her sister's wooded property in Tennessee. Unable to drive or work fulltime, Marty still suffers residual damage from an aneurysm at age 30 that left her unable to care for her two young sons. Fortunately, her ex-husband kept the boys. She lived off and on with parents and friends for several years, then finally alone, until enough of her memory came back to support herself with occasional landscaping or domestic work. She tried a full-time job with the state food-stamp program once, but found the stress too much to continue. Combating a constant struggle to remember lyrics, her musical talent also landed her an occasional low-paying gig with local bands. Today she barely plays her guitar due to an increasing lack of concentration. She also battles agoraphobia.

Families In Transition

Another factor contributing to demand for long-term care is that the caregiving system in the home has experienced a significant decline. The bulk of caregiving is performed by women,[31] and over 61% of the women in the United States are employed full

*name has been changed to protect anonymity

or part-time.[32] Dr. Ken Dychtwald, an expert on the aging population, projects that the average 21st century American will actually spend more years caring for parents than children.[33] In fact, a Princeton, New Jersey-based employee assistance firm predicts that by the year 2005, elder care will replace child care as the #1 dependent care need, as 1 out of 3 workers will be caring for an aging parent.[34]

Often the need to care for aging parents coincides with the need to pay college tuition for dependent children. Even if college tuition needs are satisfied, the "empty nest" becomes filled with frail parents or in-laws and saving for retirement is compromised. The conflicting priorities for the ways both money and time are spent have to be carefully weighed. A recent study found that 12 percent of families who help elderly relatives dip into college funds and 26 percent use money allocated for retirement to pay for this care.[35]

Also, children now live extended distances from parents as our society becomes increasingly mobile. The impact of this mobility? Today, less than 15% of people over 65 live with relatives. The rest live independently, either alone or with a spouse.[36]

Of course, it is only fair to recognize that sometimes we simply cannot be cared for at home due to physical or mental conditions, even when someone is at home to provide the care. An Alzheimer's patient, for example, usually requires 24 hour care, which is extremely difficult for most families to manage.

Forty-one-year-old Julie Endert of Murfreesboro, Tennessee, quit a job she loved with the local school system to care for her aging father, who suffers from dementia. Her decision to quit was undoubtedly influenced by her husband and two teenaged children, one in college. Her only respite time to do grocery shopping and run other errands is made possible by an adult day care program that cares for her father three days a week.[37]

Since almost half of nursing home patients have some type of dementia,[38] this may help explain why a national survey showed that 55% of severely disabled people with both spouse and children receive some formal care.[39] So even though you and your children may want you to live with them when you need long-term care, it's just not always possible when you need continuous caregiving 24 hours a day. On the other hand, if you require lighter caregiving, a home health aide may be able to stay with you for an eight- to ten-hour shift while your children work. This assistance can postpone and even eliminate entering a nursing home for some people.

But few Americans realize how precious a few hours a day of home health care can be to a distraught, exhausted caregiver until they are in the situation themselves, and even fewer Americans realize that those few hours which may mean the difference between sanity and insanity, to quote one caregiver, are not covered by health insurance. Consider these real-life situations:

A rare neurological disorder called primary lateral sclerosis has robbed Gary Nulty at age 43 of his ability to walk or feed himself. His 41-year-old wife and childhood sweetheart, Vivian, has lost 30 pounds in the past year trying to care for him and their two daughters. An environmental geologist, Gary had excellent health insurance, but just as with other health insurance plans, it will not pay custodial care. Gary's mental capacity is excellent, but he cannot even pick up the telephone or right himself in his wheelchair if he slumps over. Vivian manages a part-time job, which she desperately needs since Gary can no longer work, so that he is alone only about two hours a day until their 11-year-old daughter gets home from school. Otherwise she provides him with constant care, since he can't even go to the bathroom by himself. Vivian is desperate for help. "There's 24 hours in a day," she said. "I'm willing to work 20. I'll take four [hours of help]. That's the minimum I need to not go insane."[40]

Actress Emma Thompson (Sense and Sensibility, Howard's End) helped her mother and sister care for her actor/writer/director father Eric Thompson, after his stroke in her teens. With a combined family effort, he was able to live until age 52, which meant about 15 years of caregiving. The good side, Emma notes, is it caused her and her sister to skip the normal teenage rebellion years because her mom needed so much help.[41]

The Caregiver's Glass Ceiling

Women own 38% of all businesses and one out of 3 small businesses, and that's where the real growth is. Between 1994 and 1998, companies with 20 or less employees generated nearly 9 million jobs, representing about 80% of all new jobs created. For all size companies, women employ 27 million people, over 20% of the total work force.[42] It's fair to say, women have made monumental progress in the workforce in the last twenty or so years. What can stop them now?

Caregiving can slow and even stop many talented women. Since three-fourths of caregivers are women and two-thirds of these women work outside the home, caregiving may turn out to be the biggest threat to the women's movement in this century. The average amount of time that caregivers spend caring for someone who needs help with two or more Activities of Daily Living (bathing, dressing, transferring, eating, etc.) is 56.5 hours per week. Sixty-four percent of these most intense caregivers had to make changes to their daily work schedule to accommodate caregiving. Ultimately, 30% had to give up work entirely, 15% took early retirement and 26% had to take a leave of absence.[43]

How do you function in an executive position or grow your own business with those kinds of hours?

Technology and Lifestyle

A benefit from enhanced medical technology is increased survival from medical disorders such as heart attack, diabetes, brain tumors . . . things that 30 years ago people would have died from. A downside to prolonging life for these individuals is they may now be at risk of stroke. Stroke is the third leading cause of death in the United States, but is the #1 cause of disability.[44]

And as much as we like to think that we have healthier lifestyles, obesity is rampant in America. The risk of stroke is exacerbated when obesity is combined with one or more health problems such as high blood pressure or high cholesterol or lifestyle choices such as smoking or lack of exercise.

Competing with the highest demand for long-term care ever experienced in the United States is the low level of financing available for long-term care.

Together, conventional health insurance and Medicare pay less than a fourth of the nation's bill for home health care and nursing home care of greater than $117 billion annually, and that small payment is mostly for short-term care that lasts less than three months, not long-term care which can last several years.[45]

Why Doesn't Private Insurance Pay More?

Conventional insurance, including individual and group health insurance for people under 65 or retiree health plans restrict coverage to **SKILLED CARE**—and that's why conventional health insurance does not pay for long-term care, as was illustrated in the real-life stories of younger people needing long-term care in the previous section, *Families in Transition.* HMOs, the new managed care programs for people of all ages, are even more restrictive than regular health insurance and pay very little for home health and nursing home care.

What is meant by skilled care? *Skilled care has nothing to do with how sick you are.* A person can be totally paralyzed or in a coma and still not be receiving skilled care, in which case private insurance will not pay. Skilled care is care to get you better— IVs, dressing bedsores, providing physical and speech therapy after a stroke, etc. Once progress stops, however, the care is "chronic," or "maintenance" and is no longer skilled. Daily cleaning of a colostomy drain or a catheter, or even oxygen or respiratory therapy needed regularly for an emphysema patient, are examples of care that is not skilled. Here's a real-life example of a family who did not understand the concept of skilled care at all:

The once-vibrant 39-year-old Guity Manteghi lies in a nursing home in Walnut Creek, California. Her heart failed with no warning in January, 1996, cutting off oxygen to her brain and sending her into a coma. After eight weeks, the insurance plan said she no longer needed skilled care and stopped payment to the nursing home the next day. With two young daughters, the 50-year-old husband, Maleck Manteghi, doesn't know where to turn. "I thought I had the most adequate health coverage you could buy," he is quoted in the Contra Costa Times *as saying, "When you get insurance, who knows what custodial care is, what skilled nursing is?"*[46] (Editor's note: Mrs. Manteghi passed away in 1997.)

Why Doesn't Medicare Pay More?

Medicare can approve up to 100 days in a nursing home but patients usually collect less. Why? Because Medicare pays only for *skilled* care and the majority of nursing home care is not skilled. In fact, **the average number of days that patients collect for Medicare for nursing home care is only about 23 days,** because most people don't have very many days that qualify as skilled care under Medicare guidelines.[47] Medicare pays nothing for eight-hour shifts at home and only pays home health care visits, when some skilled care is being done. An Alzheimer's patient is a classic example of someone who needs little or no skilled care and would likely not benefit from Medicare. Medicare supplements and Medicare HMOs won't pay a dime unless Medicare pays first, so they won't pay either.

Due to recent legislation to promote cost containment in the Medicare program, restricted access to Medicare payments for home health care and nursing home care is expected to continue. (See *Medicare Benefits* in **Appendix A.**)

As you can see, a 30-year-old with private health insurance is not much better off for long-term care than an 80-year-old on Medicare.

You Can't Count on Medicaid

Medicaid, the federal and state welfare program for the poor, pays almost 40% of the annual bill, and almost one-third comes out of private pockets—maybe yours.[48] It is easy to get Medicaid if you're almost broke. About a quarter of the patients paid for by Medicaid did not enter a nursing home on Medicaid.[49] They spent down, exhausted their resources, then became Medicaid patients as described on p. 129.

You should beware of anyone who advises you to transfer assets to your children or trusts in order to qualify for Medicaid. Children may misuse or lose the assets (i.e., in the event of a lawsuit or divorce). Also, many nursing homes no longer accept Medicaid patients because a Medicaid patient represents a financial loss to most nursing homes. A Medicaid patient is at the mercy of the system and may have nowhere to go if nursing homes are full, or may have to go to a rural area if urban homes are full. It's not unusual for a Medicaid patient to be placed hours away from family members. Denise Gott, an Ohio insurance agent, related this story of a family who found this out the hard way:

I conducted a workshop for a AAA Club in Canton, Ohio in September of 1999. I had finished the program and was tak-

ing questions. A young gentleman in his late thirties sitting with his wife raised his hand and asked if he could share a story. He proceeded to explain to the crowd of about 40 people that both his mother and father were in nursing homes; they had been there for 2 and 4 years respectively. Unfortunately for this family, they spent nearly all of their assets on the first two years of nursing home care for the father. When the mother went into the nursing home, the family home was sold, the remaining assets totaling $50,000 and the income that the mother was receiving from her retirement plan were all redirected to the nursing home to pay expenses. All funds ran out after the first year and a half that Mom was in the facility. To make matters worse, both parents are now on Medicaid. The saddest part of this story is that due to the fact that there are very few available Medicaid beds in Ohio, Mom lives in a nursing home in Cleveland while Dad lives in a nursing facility in Toledo, a full two hours away. The couple lives in Canton, making visits to both nursing facilities difficult, both physically and emotionally.

Also, in most states, being on Medicaid means being in a nursing home. The option for home care is eliminated because most Medicaid programs pay very little for home health care and nothing for eight hour shifts in the home. Less than 17% of home care costs in 1998 were paid by Medicaid.[50] To have options for home care, assisted living, adult day care, and to be able to choose any nursing home, a number of adult children are purchasing long-term care insurance policies for parents, even though financially the parents will either immediately or in a short time qualify for Medicaid.

A 69-year-old woman and her 30-year-old daughter cer-
tainly felt that way. When my client purchased her policy in
1993, her only asset outside of her home was a $30,000
annuity and she was a widow. Her daughter attended the
appointment and expressed how strongly she felt about keep-
ing her mother off Medicaid if at all possible. We all cried
around the kitchen table with the emotion of planning
ahead for something no one wanted to happen, but if it did,
that night's action of purchasing a long-term care insurance
policy would make the way a lot easier by providing money
to pay for choices that would make nursing home care a last
resort.

Prospects for Government Help

Because of the serious nature of the long-term care crisis, some
people advocate that a new benefit program be created by the
federal government to pay for long-term care for everyone.

The answer to this question arrived in 1996 with a new health
care reform package that provides tax incentives for individuals
and employers to purchase long-term care insurance. Basically,
the government is saying there isn't enough money for any type
of public program to pay for long-term care for everyone.

Consider that in 1945, in the early days of the Social Security
program, there were 40 workers for each retiree. In 1995, the
ratio was 3.4 workers for every Social Security beneficiary. By
2040, the ratio is projected to decline to 2 to 1.[51] With costs of
home health and nursing home care more than $117 billion
per year and expected to increase at least five times in the next

30 years, from where will the taxes originate to pay the tab? We are already spending 44 cents of every federal income tax dollar on entitlements, primarily the "Big Three": Social Security, Medicare and Medicaid.[52] A long-term care program for the 76 million baby boomers would be a larger entitlement than these existing programs, which are already facing insolvency.

Recent Health Care Reform

To encourage Americans to plan for their own long-term care needs and to ensure that long-term care insurance has great value for the future, the federal government has passed legislation to provide tax incentives for long-term care insurance policies issued on and after January 1, 1997,* and to standardize the benefits somewhat to offer the best value for the consumer. For "qualified" policies that meet these criteria, the following apply for 2001:

▲   Benefits will not be taxable income, as long as benefit payments above $200 per day (or the monthly equivalent) do not exceed the actual cost of care. Conversely, benefit payments in excess of $200 per day that do exceed the actual cost of care will be taxed as income.

▲   A portion of a long-term care insurance premium based on the age of the policyholder now counts as a medical expense. Since medical expenses in excess of 7½% of adjusted gross income are tax deductible, this means that a portion of your long-term care insurance premium will help you reach that threshold and may

---

* Policies purchased 12/31/96 and earlier were "grandfathered" and are considered qualified for the new tax treatment. Also, this section is not intended in any way to give tax advice. Please see your tax advisor for a final determination of how this legislation applies to you.

even put you over it to receive a tax deduction. Here are the amounts that count, and they are allowed to increase each year based on the medical Consumer Price Index:

Age at End of Taxable Year	Amount of LTC Insurance Premium That Counts as a Medical Expense in:	
	2000	2001
40 and younger	$220	$230
41–50	$410	$430
51–60	$820	$860
61–70	$2,200	$2,290
71 and older	$2,750	$2,860

While younger people generally don't have enough medical expenses to gain a tax deduction from long-term care insurance premiums, this provision may make it worthwhile for older Americans to itemize.

Let's look at an example. Bob is 74 and Martha is 71. Their long-term care insurance premiums are $3,200 and $2,800 respectively. Based on the above table for the year 2000, they each get to count $2,750 of the premium as a medical expense, for a total of $5,500. They have an additional $4,500 in other medical expenses for retiree health insurance premiums and their deductibles and co-payments for that plan. Together with the $5,500 deduction for their long-term care insurance premium, they have $10,000 in total medical expenses. For tax purposes, they can count the amount of medical expense that exceeds 7½ % of their adjusted gross income. Their income is $50,000 and 7½ % is $3,750, so they can count $6,250 in medical expenses.

They also have $1,500 in charitable contributions and $2,900 in state and property taxes, so their total itemized deductions equal $10,650. Since this exceeds the standard deduction of $9,050 for 2000, they are better off to itemize. Combined with the personal exemption of $2,800 per person that everyone is entitled to, their total deductions equal $16,250 ($2,800 x 2 = $5,600 + $10,650). Therefore their taxable income is lowered from $50,000 to $33,750. If they just took the standard deduction of $9,050 and didn't itemize, their taxable income would be $35,350. The difference of $1,600 in a 15% tax bracket means they will save $240 in income tax. (See chart on next page)

IRS-Approved Medical Expenses

It is surprising how many things count as a medical expense in the eyes of the IRS. A partial list includes: contact lenses, eyeglasses, hearing aids, false teeth, artificial limbs, wheelchairs, oxygen and oxygen equipment, prescription drugs and insulin, medical and hospital insurance premiums, cost and care of guide dogs or other animals aiding the blind, deaf, and disabled, medical fees from doctors, dentists, surgeons, specialists, and other medical practitioners, hospital fees, wages and certain taxes for nursing services for chronically ill people, transportation for needed medical care, stop-smoking programs, meals and lodging provided by a hospital during medical treatment. Contact your local Social Security office for a complete list.

	With LTC Insurance	Without LTC Insurance
Adjusted Gross Income for Married Couple	50,000	50,000
Personal Exemptions	5,600	5,600
Itemized Deductions:		
Medical Expense	6,250	750
Charitable Contributions	1,500	1,500
Taxes	2,900	2,900
Total Itemized	10,650	5,150
Standard Deduction	9,050	9,050
Total Deductions from AGI	16,250	14,650
Taxable Income	33,750	35,350
Marginal Federal Rate	15%	15%
Total Federal Taxes	5,063	5,303

Tax savings with LTC insurance = $240

▲   The allowable percentage of an LTC insurance premium is now treated like a health insurance premium for the self-employed tax deduction, which provides a first-dollar tax deduction of 60% for tax years 1999-2001, 70% for 2002 and 100% for tax years 2003 and beyond. "Self-employed" means sole proprietors, partnerships and "greater than 2% shareholders" of S-Corporations and Limited Liability Corporations.

Mary owns an S-Corporation, so she is considered self-employed by the IRS. Her health insurance premium is

$1,500 per year and her long-term care insurance is $1,000 per year. Based on her age of 48, she is allowed to add $430 of her long-term care insurance premium to her $1,500 health insurance premium for a total premium of $1,930, of which she will receive 60% as a first-dollar tax deduction for tax year 2001. Sixty percent of $1,930 is $1,158, so her adjusted gross income for 2001 will be lowered by that amount.

▲ Employers who are defined as a C-corporation will receive a tax deduction for any portion of the long-term care insurance premiums paid for employees, regardless of ownership in the company. Other employers who are self-employed (see previous bullet) must count a long-term care insurance premium as part of their salary. This makes it taxable income if they allow the premium to be paid by the business, and deductible only in the form of salary or compensation.

Premium paid for their employees, on the other hand, does not count as income for the employees and the entire premium is 100% deductible as a business expense to the company. Even though it has to be counted as taxable income, some self-employed owners want the business to pay the premium for cash-flow purposes, and they do still get the first-dollar self-employed deduction described in the preceding bullet, which will be 100% by tax year 2003.

▲ Premium contributions made by all types of employers will not be taxable income to employees.

▲   Long-term care insurance premiums are an acceptable medical expense under the new Medical Savings Account (MSA) experiment for the first 750,000 workers who set them up and who are either self-employed or who work for small businesses with 50 employees or less. The experiment ran through 2000 but has been extended two more years. Hopefuly MSA's will apply to companies of all sizes in the future. Check with a health insurance agent for specific availability in your area, but here's a general description of how it works (the dollar amounts cited below for 2000 are subject to change each year):

Individuals must purchase a deductible of $1,550–$2,350 and families must purchase a $3,100–$4,650 deductible. Individuals can put 65% of the deductible into the MSA, and families are allowed to deposit 75% of the family deductible. MSA's are funded with pretax dollars, and unused money at the end of the year grows tax-deferred—this is not a "use it or lose it" model. Funds can be used at age 65 for any reason without penalty. Prior to age 65, a 15% penalty is imposed for funds withdrawn for other than an acceptable medical expense (see a partial list of IRS-approved medical expenses on p. 21.) Premiums are typically 30%–50% lower than managed care or traditional health insurance plans. (The contribution can be made by either the employer or employee, but not in combination. Therefore some employers pay the MSA premium, then make a savings contribution into each employee's account equaling the difference between the MSA premium and the amount that would otherwise have been paid for health care coverage.)

▲ Long-term care insurance can also be paid from Medical Savings Accounts for tax years 1999–2003 established by the first 390,000 Medicare beneficiaries. For specific information on how the program works, and how to determine availability in your local area, see *Managed Care Medicare Plans* in **Appendix A.**

▲ Unreimbursed expenses for "qualified" long-term care **services**—the cost of long-term care itself, not LTC insurance premiums—will count toward the itemized medical deduction, if paid on behalf of yourself, your spouse or your dependents. (See *Claims* in the next chapter for a definition of "qualified" care.)

This means unreimbursed "qualified" care, as well as long-term care insurance premiums that you pay for a parent, will count as long as you contribute more than 50% of your parent's support. The allowable portion of long-term care insurance premiums that count is based on the parent's age, not yours. Sometimes children form a "multiple support agreement," which means collectively they provide more than 50% of a parent's support. In this case, one child each year can take the tax deduction as long as that child individually provides at least 10% of the parent's support.

▲ Certain benefit provisions are required, which will be discussed in the next chapter, **Features of a Good Long-Term Care Insurance Policy.**

What is this law really saying? The message is loud and clear: **Take care of your long-term care needs with private insurance,** because there isn't enough money to create a new entitlement program for everyone.

Apparently many states agree. The following states have implemented state tax incentives for long-term care insurance: AL, CA, CO, HI, IL, IN, IA, KY, ME, MD, MN, MO, MT, OH, OR, NY, NC, ND, UT, VA, WV, and WI. Several states offer private long-term care insurance to state employees. The Federal Employee Program plans to join the surge in the next couple of years as the largest employer in the nation to offer private long-term care insurance.

The Balanced Budget Act of 1997 implemented several drastic changes in the Medicare skilled nursing facility and home health benefit that will result in restricted access to these benefits for many years to come. (The Balanced Budget Refinement Act of 1999 and the Medicare and Medicaid Benefits Improvement and Protection Act of 2000 restored some of the funds that were taken away by the original act, but some say the amount restored may not be enough.) Legislation like this makes LTC policies more meaningful as government shifts costs away from Medicare to private LTC insurance.

The Private Sector Solution

Almost 7 million Americans have turned to private long-term care plans to protect their assets.[53] Over 3000 employers offer group long-term care coverage, and the number of employer plans in force has tripled in five years.[54] With new tax incentives for employers, this trend should continue to explode in the 21st century. Many buyers are in their 40's and 50's as most insurance companies target these age groups with attractively low premiums. Long-term care insurance is the private sector's solution to what an increasing number of people are calling "the *real* health care crisis" in the United States. Right now, private health insurance only pays 7% of long-term care costs, and welfare (Medicaid) is paying almost 40%.[55] If private long-term care insurance doesn't flip those percentages for the baby-boomer generation, the tax consequences to all of us will be unprecedented. Most importantly, long-term care insurance for many represents the best opportunity to retain a sense of dignity—in the form of purchasing power—which all too many people who thought they were affluent have lost to the merciless financial demands of long-term care.

People who are not affluent also are buying long-term care insurance. Fifty percent of purchasers in 2000 had assets less than $100,000, and almost two-thirds had an income of less than $35,000.[56] These statistics are not so surprising when you look at the most frequently cited reasons for purchasing the insurance—**to maintain independence and choice** by guaranteeing affordability of care in order to avoid depending on others for care. Asset protection was only the third most important reason for purchase.[57]

Based on today's current economic environment with lower investment earnings, it is strongly advisable for individuals to consider LTC insurance when their asset base ranges between $50,000 and $2 million, not counting the home and automobile. *Fortune* magazine reports:

> *In fact, for anyone with a household income ranging from $40,000 to $250,000 . . . there's long-term care insurance or nothing.*[58]

A prominent national group of financial planners who specialize in wealth preservation and wealth transfer extends the asset figure to $5 million for its clients. Many people in the "several million" asset range plan to self-insure their long-term care risk. If you are in this category and self-insuring is a viable option, you may want to seriously consider the single premium/life insurance or annuity LTC policies, since these types of policies will pass any money you don't use for long-term care on to the beneficiary of your choice (heirs, church, charity, your estate, etc.), but if you do need long-term care, your dollars are maximized for long-term care coverage. (See **Alternatives for Financing Long-Term Care,** p. 151, for a description.)

It's difficult to box appropriate purchasers for long-term care insurance into a range of assets and income, because people buy things for different reasons. Consider this story:

> *David Miller, an Ohio insurance agent, sold long-term care insurance to a man who owns ten McDonald's. Mr. Miller was understandably shocked that this gentleman wished to purchase insurance and asked why. With tears in his eyes, the client pointed to an oil painting of a young man, and said, "That's my reason for wanting to do this. That is our son who was killed in an automobile accident 17 years ago and I want to make sure his children will be taken care of for college and someday buying their own homes, and I want to take care of my other kids and grandkids. I don't want one dime of my money ever going to a nursing home!" Mr. Miller understood quickly that here was a man who was determined to spend his money on his family just as much as it was in his control to do so and sold him and his wife long-term care insurance policies.*

People with larger estates especially need to determine the amount of liquid assets that can be used upon demand. Otherwise a long-term care need may require the sale of investments or property at a loss. If you are "house rich and cash poor," you may want to consider a reverse mortgage, which will allow you to leverage the money from your home to pay for long-term care insurance instead of paying premiums out of the income you use for living expenses. (See **Reverse Mortgages,** p. 174.)

But think about it, affluent people don't usually spend their own money when they don't have to. Seventy-five percent of Americans over 65 have private health insurance in addition to Medicare, at a time when there is very little left to pay after Medicare pays. The average out-of-pocket expense, excluding home care and nursing home expenses, for someone with no supplemental insurance of any type to Medicare is less than $2,000.[59]

Affluent people also have homeowners' policies even when the mortgage is paid off, yet the odds of needing long-term care, at 1 out of 2 are much higher than losing a home. Just think, if you looked out of your window and saw one out of two houses burning in your neighborhood! We can't sleep at night without a homeowners' policy, yet losses for long-term care can be much greater than the cost of replacing our house. This is probably why an educational insert in a recent issue of *Fortune* magazine contained a highlighted block that said:

Long-term care is more important than car and homeowners insurance, since the statistical probability of using it is higher.[60]

People with assets greater than $50,000 who believe in Medicare supplement policies and homeowners' policies are well advised to consider long-term care insurance. This means that the $500,000 or more they might spend on long-term care could go to a favorite charity, church or be split among the grandchildren.

The following chart shows that a couple with $500,000 will spend down to nothing in less than six years, with only one spouse needing long-term care at almost $50,000 per year. Another consideration is that affluent people may be interested in around-the-clock home health care, which can triple these costs.

Year	Assets at Start of Year	Income Needs	LTC Expense	Investment Yield	Assets at End of Year
1	$500,000	$59,703	$48,914	$40,000	$431,384
2	431,384	61,494	51,359	34,511	353,042
3	353,042	63,339	53,927	28,243	264,019
4	264,019	65,239	56,623	21,122	163,279
5	163,279	67,196	59,455	13,062	49,691
6	49,691	69,212	62,427	3,975	-77,973

Note: "Income Needs" is the portion of household income needs that the assets had been relied upon to provide and assumes annual inflation of 3%. "LTC Expense" is for nursing home care, based on a typical rate, and is subject to 5% annual inflation. "Investment Yield" is assumed at 8% annually after taxes.

People with lower assets are purchasing long-term care insurance to maintain independence and receive the same treatment as private pay patients if care is needed, or their children are buying it for them for the same reason.

Most of us can imagine the consequences of walking into a hospital or doctor's office with no health insurance! Mary Vanac of the *Akron Beacon Journal* writes, "That's why many legal and financial professionals are advising their middle-aged clients to plan for their own long-term care, as well as for the care of their parents, and such planning involves the whole family . . . Although it's a hard topic to broach, planning for long-term care can keep a tough family situation from becoming a disastrous one."[61]

Margie White of Plano, Texas, bought a long-term care policy at the advice of Joan Gruber, a Dallas financial planner who specializes in helping adult children with aging parents, after caring for both parents and losing her marriage as a result. "There was a definite lack of foresight and planning on my parents' part," she says. "I can understand. They never expected to live that long. But it took five or six years out of my life. I don't want my sons to have to do this for me."[62]

Parents who buy long-term care insurance are taking care of their children far into the future. As many caregivers can attest, caregiving takes a phenomenal toll mentally, physically and even spiritually. Exhausted caregivers may become care recipients themselves, leading to a further, often preventable, drain on resources. Carol Levine, a nurse who has been caring for her husband, who is totally disabled and requires 24-hour care after a severe brain-stem injury in a car accident ten years ago, wonders, "Does my managed-care company realize that during the past year it paid more for my stress-related medical problems than for my husband's medical care?"

In addition to accidents and other traumas that cause younger people to need long-term care, our rapidly aging population is putting insupportable demands on families in this century. Families simply can't shoulder this monumental burden alone. They have to have help.

LTC insurance means choices and options when that help is needed. For most of us, long-term care insurance may be the main key to not outliving our money—a very real fear that a number of people have as life spans continue to increase.

Chapter 2

Features of a Good Long-Term Care Insurance Policy

〜〜〜〜〜〜〜〜〜〜〜〜〜〜〜〜〜〜〜〜〜〜〜〜〜〜〜

E ffective January 1, 1997, new health care legislation required insurance companies to offer new "tax-qualified" policies that contain certain standardized benefits that were recommended by the National Association of Insurance Commissioners (NAIC), the regulatory body composed of all of the state insurance commissioners. Most of these guidelines were already being followed by the insurance companies and simply provide extra protection for the consumer to ensure high value for premium dollars.

Congress ruled that long-term care policies issued prior to 1/1/97 will count as qualified policies and do not have to be exchanged for a new policy. This includes employer-sponsored plans that were set up prior to 1/1/97, so that new enrollees after 1/1/97 have a "grandfathered" plan. However, if you materially change a policy that you purchased prior to 1/1/97, the policy will lose this "grandfathered" status and will no longer be considered tax-qualified by the IRS. An example of a "material change" would be adding an inflation rider, which is a benefit increase for additional premium. A partial list of changes that are not considered a material change and therefore would not affect the grandfathered status are:

▲ Premium modal changes; e.g., changing an annual payment to monthly payments.

▲ A class rate increase or decrease, which means a rate increase or decrease that applies to an entire segment of policyholders.

▲ Discounts that you receive after the original issue date of your policy due to other family members purchasing a policy; for example, if your spouse purchases a policy at a later date than you do.

▲ Premium decreases due to a reduction in coverage:

▲ Provision of alternate forms of benefits that do not increase the premium; for example, companies sometimes add coverage for new forms of care, like assisted living, without increasing your premium.

▲ Allowing policyholders to continue group coverage if the policyholder is no longer part of the group; for example, because he or she terminates employment with an employer who offered a group long-term care insurance plan.

(*Caution:* Some insurance companies are still marketing non-qualified policies. Please be aware that if you purchased a non-qualified policy in 1997 or later, there is a chance that the IRS will say that benefits received from the non-qualified policy will be taxable income to you. A quick way to see if your policy is tax-qualified is to check the first page of your policy. All tax-qualified policies issued after 1/1/97 have a sentence that says the policy is intended to satisfy the requirements for a tax-qualified policy. As you read this chapter, you also will learn how to check the benefits to ensure that you have a tax-qualified policy.)

To provide you with a measuring stick for value if you already have a long-term care insurance policy or if you are currently shopping for a policy, this section will explain each feature of a long-term care policy in detail to give you an in-depth understanding of how long-term care insurance works. If you are shopping for a policy, you will find helpful recommendations for appropriate benefit selections that you can apply to your situation. An insurance agent who sells long-term care insurance can help you finalize your choices.

Level of Care

Make sure the policy pays all levels of care—skilled or non-skilled—in any setting: the home, in an assisted living facility, in an adult day care center, or in a nursing home. (Sometimes you will hear non-skilled referred to as intermediate or custodial care. "Intermediate" means some skilled care but not every day, and "custodial" means no skilled care at all. These terms are old and just refer to non-skilled care.) Benefits should not be reduced because the level of care is less than skilled. Also, the policy should not require skilled care before non-skilled benefits are paid.

Home Health Care

About 1.5 million people are in nursing homes[1] and about 10 million are being cared for at home or in a community setting like assisted living or adult day care,[2] so less than 15% of long-term care is in a nursing home. The number of nursing home patients has actually declined in recent years due to an increased availability of home health and other community services. Understandably, coverage for home health is a popular addition to long-term care insurance policies. Here are some points to keep in mind when choosing a policy:

▲   The home health care benefit is not intended to be 24-hour per day home health care because around-the-clock care at home is more expensive than nursing home care. The home care benefit is most helpful when you have someone to live with; i.e. a "primary caregiver," such as a spouse, son, daughter, or other family member or friend. If you qualify for benefits under the policy, a home health aide can stay with you for an eight- to ten-hour shift while your primary caregiver is at work, for example. The aide can do the heavy caregiving, such as giving you a bath (something you may not want a family member to do), washing your hair, changing your bed, preparing meals, supervising your medicine, and maybe light housework and laundry. Then perhaps your family can take care of you at night. Even if you have a primary caregiver who doesn't work, no one can provide 24-hour care, so home health care can make it possible for your primary caregiver to get adequate rest.

A common statement is "I'm not buying long-term care insurance because I'm never going to a nursing home."

The irony is that a long-term care policy with great home health benefits may be the only thing that keeps you out of a nursing home by providing financial and emotional support to the people who care about you so they can keep you at home.

Judy Geck, Chattanooga, Tennessee, has seen both of her parents in long-term care. Her father had a major stroke six years ago, which was magnified by complications from the diabetes he had suffered with since his early 40's. After almost two years of caregiving, he passed away within weeks prior to being admitted to a nursing home. Her mother had a severe stroke three months after his death which, coupled with dementia, made it necessary for her to move in with Judy and her husband, Richard. Having a very solid position with the same company over fifteen years, Judy was loathe to give up her job for financial reasons, especially since she had a new grandchild to buy for! In order to keep her demanding job and get adequate rest at night, it has been necessary to have home health aides 16 hours a day, from 7 A.M. till 11 P.M. Judy sleeps in a chair four nights a week next to her mother and has an additional home health aide the other three nights.

It's been four years since the stroke, and her mother still can't be left alone. In addition to the dementia, she is unable to speak and cannot respond to verbal commands to move her body due to damaged motor skills from the stroke. Judy is home every evening and activities or even vacation ideas that would take her away from home have been out of the question. The time when the paid home care is cut back, and her mother's savings run out, could be as soon as a year.

▲   If you want to design your policy to pay 24-hour home care, work with your insurance agent to determine the cost for that service in your community so you can select a daily or monthly benefit that is high enough to accomplish your goal. This selection will substantially increase the premium.

▲ Home health coverage is automatically included in some policies—these policies are usually called "integrated" policies—and optional in other policies. If the coverage is optional and you really have no one to live with when you need care, you might consider putting your premium dollars toward a policy that covers just assisted living and nursing home benefits. You can use the premium that you would have spent on home health benefits to buy a higher daily benefit to help you afford a private room, for example, or a longer benefit period such as five years or even a lifetime (unlimited) benefit period.

▲ There are a handful of policies that pay only for home health care with no coverage for assisted living or nursing home care. No policy can guarantee that you will never need nursing home care, so a policy that focuses 100% on home care may not be a wise choice. (It's doubtful that very many of the 1.5 million Americans in nursing homes today "planned" to be there!)

▲ The most valuable home health benefit pays the same level of benefit for home care as for nursing home care, or at least 75%-80%, instead of paying home care at a lower amount such as 50% of the nursing home benefit, as many policies offer. Why? Because an eight-hour shift of home health care costs almost the same as a semi-private day in a nursing home.

▲ If the policy allows family and friends to provide the care, a lower benefit can work since these people may charge less. (A policy like this has a higher premium, but will pay a monthly benefit to you, and you can hire anyone you like, or use the money for other needs. If you hire caregivers and pay them yourself, the IRS probably will view you as an employer. Your accountant can help you understand any employer responsibilities you may have in this capacity.)

▲ Some policies, however, require care to be provided by a licensed home health care agency and do not pay for family and friends (unless the family member is a licensed health care professional and services are billed through a third party, such as a home health agency).

▲ Many policies do not require that the care be provided through a home health agency. A policy like this will pay "professionals operating within the scope of their license," such as a Registered Nurse (RN) or Licensed Practical Nurse (LPN) who is freelancing his or her services. It is possible to find a policy that will pay for a family member, friend, or other person of your choice, except for an immediate family member, to obtain the necessary license or certification in your state to be paid as a freelancer. This can be helpful if you live in a rural area without a strong network of home health care agencies. (To find out more about your state's home care licensing and certification training program, call your state's Agency on Aging in **Appendix B** of this book and ask for the telephone number of your state's association for home health professionals.)

▲   To help family members who are willing to be free care-givers, most policies pay for caregiver training to teach a family member how to provide care in the most effec-tive and safest way for both patient and caregiver; e.g., lifting techniques, patient positioning to avoid pressure sores, insulin injections, changing bandages, and so forth. The benefit amount for this feature is usually five times the daily benefit.

▲   The policy should not require a nursing home stay prior to providing coverage for home health care.

▲   The policy should pay for non-skilled care at home (bathing, dressing, helping the patient get in and out of bed, etc.) with no requirement for skilled care (care performed by nurses, physical therapists, speech thera-pists, etc.) Some policies also pay for companion care.

▲   The policy should cover adult day care in addition to home health care.

Assisted Living

Sometimes people may need help with one or two Activities of Daily Living (ADL), such as bathing or dressing, but may not need total 24-hour care in a nursing home. Retirement centers and nursing homes often have special sections for people who need just slight assistance. This type of assistance is called "assisted living." This type of care also is available in some independent facilities such as personal care homes or bed and board homes. Assisted living is a popular form of long-term care because the setting is more like a home setting and costs less than nursing home care. (Compare the cost of about $73.50 a day for assisted living vs. $131 a day for semi-private nursing home care, both for just room and board—miscellaneous charges like drugs and medical supplies will bump both figures up about 20%.)[3,4]

Assisted living is a wonderful alternative to nursing home care and consequently may be the fastest growing form of long-term care. To further explain the difference, nursing home residents typically need help with 3–4 Activities of Daily Living, while assisted living residents only need help with 1–2 ADLs and are certainly not bed bound. So assisted living provides a place that looks like independent living to many people who can't stay home anymore because they need extra help. Also, assisted living facilities make it possible for spouses to remain together, whereas nursing homes usually do not, at least in the same room.

Although many assisted living residents would not qualify for benefits under long-term care insurance policies because they don't need very much help, the Assisted Living Federation of America reports that about half of assisted living residents need help with two or more Activities of Daily Living and probably would qualify.[5] Others may qualify under the cognitive impairment benefit trigger as the same report says that almost half of the residents have some form of cognitive impairment.

Many policies provide assisted living benefits at a percentage of the nursing home benefit, and some provide equal benefits.

Some policies pay assisted living under the nursing home benefit and some under the home health care benefit. If you want the assisted living coverage and you are considering a "nursing home only" policy, make sure the assisted living benefit is paid under the nursing home benefit vs. the home health care benefit.

Guaranteed Renewable

Make sure the policy cannot be cancelled as long as premiums are paid, even if the insurance company stops selling long-term care insurance.

Prior Hospitalization

It is illegal today to sell a policy that won't pay nursing home benefits without a prior hospital stay. Many older policies were sold with this restriction, and their premiums are lower because these policies screen out a large number of claims. With strict hospital admission guidelines set forth by private insurance and Medicare, doctors can no longer admit patients just to satisfy an insurance requirement such as this. For example, Alzheimer's patients or the frail elderly usually do not need hospitalization.

Daily or Monthly Benefit

Some long-term care policies pay a flat amount per day or per month for nursing home care with selections ranging from $40–$500 per day or $1,000–$8,000 per month. Other policies will not pay more than the actual charge, regardless of the daily benefit you select. Many of these policies will allow the amount of daily benefit not used to carry over, thus extending your benefit period. Knowledge of local nursing home costs is helpful in making this selection. Costs nationwide average $157 per day for semi-private nursing home care plus prescription drugs and care-related supplies, both of which are usually billed separately from the room and board charge.[6] If home health care benefits are offered, the benefit ideally will equal the nursing home benefit but could be a percentage of the nursing home benefit, if it's at least 75%.

A policy with a monthly benefit will pay if home care for a particular day exceeds a normal daily benefit. For example, a therapist and an aide could come on the same day and charges for both might total $150. A $100 daily benefit would pay no more than $100 for that day, but a $3,000 monthly benefit would pay the entire $150 or whatever the daily charges are until the $3,000 is used up for that month. Some policies provide a weekly benefit instead of monthly for home care. This can be helpful because there is less risk of using up all of your home care benefit in the early part of the month.

Note: Some applicants intentionally select a benefit lower than area charges to merely supplement their assets and income. For example, someone with $2,100 in monthly income may figure that he would use $1,000 of his income to pay toward his care, which is the equivalent of $30 per day. He then might purchase a policy that will pay $120 per day, which results in a potential $150 per day available for an eight- to ten-hour shift of home health care or for semi-private nursing home care. Just be careful when you do this calculation to consider how much of your income you will need to pay your living expenses, which will be higher if you are receiving home care vs. nursing home care.

Some people prefer a private room and purchase a daily or monthly benefit to accommodate private room costs (i.e. $150+ daily benefit or $4,500+ monthly benefit). The daily benefit usually applies just to room and board. Additional charges, such as laundry, personal items (TV), hairdresser, etc. aren't covered, and miscellaneous charges like drugs and medical supplies can average 20% more than the room and board charges. Selecting a benefit fairly close to the average cost in your area probably means you will still be self-insuring some of the costs, especially if you have no other coverage for prescription drugs. Make sure the policy will pay the percentage of costs you expect so you won't be surprised when the bills start coming in.

The advantage of a policy that pays the daily benefit regardless of charge—an "indemnity" policy—is to provide extra money to pay for these incidental or miscellaneous charges. The advantage of a "reimbursement" policy, one that pays no more than the actual room and board charge, is to hold claim payments down and avoid rate increases for as long as possible. Since benefits above $200 per day that exceed actual costs are taxable income, most newer policies are reimbursement.

Note: A few reimbursement policies allow any difference between the daily benefit you select and the room and board charge to be used to pay miscellaneous charges that are not personal items, such as drugs and medical supplies. A couple of policies even provide a specific benefit for drugs and/or supplies.

Benefit Period/Benefit Maximum

This is the amount of time (benefit period) or money (benefit maximum) the insurance company is obligated to pay benefits.

This doesn't mean how long you can be covered. You might have your policy 15 years before you need to file a claim for benefits. After you file a claim, the benefit period is how long the insurance company is responsible to pay benefits. Benefit periods of one year to unlimited are on the market, although some states require benefit periods of at least two years to be offered. Common choices are three years, four years, five years, six years, or unlimited.

Some insurance companies express the maximum benefit in dollars instead of time. Benefit maximum usually means a specific number of days x the daily benefit you select. For example, a benefit maximum of 1,095 days x $100 daily benefit would be $109,500. This type of policy is usually a reimbursement policy. (See *Daily or Monthly Benefit* section.) If the charge happens to be less than your daily benefit, the remainder stays in this "pool of money" and extends your benefits. Instead of having the equivalent of a three-year benefit period, with the pool of $109,500 your benefits may last 3½ years or even longer. The insurance company won't stop paying benefits until all of the dollars are used. If you purchase inflation coverage, this amount usually grows each year. A few policies will allow it to grow without deducting any claim payments that were made that year.

After you have collected the maximum in benefits, the policy is over and you start paying out of your assets until you spend down to the qualifying level for Medicaid (welfare) in your state (Medi-Cal in California). A few states have a special program called The Partnership for Long-Term Care that allows you to shelter some of your assets and still qualify for Medicaid as a reward for purchasing a long-term care insurance policy. (See **The Partnership for Long-Term Care**, p. 119.)

According to recent extensive surveys, the average time caregivers report providing home care is 4.5 years, and one out of four caregivers reported providing home care longer than five years.[7]

To give you an idea of the nursing home usage, the following chart illustrates the length of stay information for 1997 patients:

Length of Stay	Percent of Nursing Home Patients
Less than 3 months	17.6%
3–6 months	9.7%
6–12 months	14.8%
1–3 yrs.	30.3%
3–5 yrs.	13.6%
5+ yrs.	14.0%

The 1997 National Nursing Home Survey, National Center for Health Statistics, U.S. Department of Health and Human Services, 7/00

The average nursing home stay is 2.4 years. Over two-thirds of nursing home patients stayed less than three years and 42% of the patients stayed less than one year. However, 14% of the patients stayed longer than five years.[8] Since women live longer than men, the majority of patients who need longer periods of care are women. Accordingly, most insurance companies will allow couples to choose different benefit periods as a way of reducing premium; i.e. a husband might choose a three-year benefit period and a wife might choose a lifetime (unlimited) benefit period.

Most caregivers are women, so men typically are taken care of at home by a wife or daughter as long as possible before entering a nursing home.[9] When a husband buys a long-term care insurance policy for himself, it may be the wife who realizes the greatest benefit from the policy because it pays for the support she needs to keep her husband at home as long as possible. On the other hand, the wife or daughter may not have a similar caregiver, and may access benefits on a long-term care policy relatively soon.

The more help a family has to provide home care, the easier it is to keep a family member at home who needs long-term care. **The money from a long-term care insurance policy may be the only thing that makes it possible to provide extended home health care for a loved one.** Cynthia Coe, an insurance agent in Massachusetts, relates what she describes as "a career transforming experience":

I received a phone call from a local life insurance agent asking me to explain the benefits of a long-term care insurance policy his client had purchased from my insurance company when he lived in another state. He had recently suffered a debilitating stroke and moved back to our town to be closer to his children.

After setting an appointment with his wife, I arrived the next day to find one of the sweetest women I have ever met in tears, absolutely distraught and exhausted. The poor woman had lost 50 pounds and was absolutely frantic because Medicare was cutting back on home care for her completely disabled husband because his condition was "not improving." Her poor husband was confined to a wheel chair or hospital bed, could not take a step, and was unable to communicate with anyone, except in a strange, garbled speech that only his wife understood. She was adamant about caring for him at home, but it was patently clear that she needed more help. I contacted the company, which immediately sent out a really nice social worker who assessed the situation and authorized benefits on the spot. We were able to arrange increased care within the week.

Three or four weeks after all this, I was having a particularly horrible day. My company was insisting I do telephone solicitation. I would rather have walked over hot coals, been caged with hungry lions, or jumped out of a plane without a parachute—and I had encountered several really nasty individuals who had sworn at me and likened me to an unethical used car salesman. In other words, despite all my belief and conviction in the importance of long-term care insurance, I HAD HAD IT! I have the heart of a social worker, not a salesperson, and my fragile little ego was quivering. But, on the way home to tell my husband that I absolutely had to find another line of work, I stopped at the bank to make a deposit, and who should be there but the wife of the client who was so disabled by the stroke. She spotted me, came rushing over, and HUGGED me with tears in her eyes and just gushed. "Thank God for you and your company, I don't know what I would have done without you." The new home care workers had given her back some semblance of a life, and she now felt she could cope with her life situation as a result of having such insurance.

Needless to say, I felt as if the Lord had given me a very strong message about the importance of the work I do. So, in spite of very regular set-backs, I still spend my days trying to spread the message about the emotional, physical, psychological and financial importance of this type of insurance—and I usually list "financial" last in this order, as the other three can eclipse every-thing else.

How long a benefit period should you purchase? The answer is, as long as you can afford, without being uncomfortable with the premium. People who take really good care of themselves, for example, may be the very people who need long episodes of long-term care. They are less likely to suffer a major heart attack or massive stroke and instead, they just wear out! The healthier they are, the longer that can take—four years, six years, ten years!

If you purchase a longer benefit period, such as lifetime (unlimited), and you decide later that it's too much premium, you can always reduce your premium by reducing your benefit period, and that's fine with the insurance company. If you start out with a shorter benefit period and decide later you want to increase it, the insurance company will require you to start over with new medical questions, and you will have to pay premium for the longer benefit period at your new age. It's in your best interest to start out with the maximum benefit period you think you might want, because you can always come down. Increasing benefits later is more expensive, and if you have developed a health problem, you may be ineligible for a benefit increase.

Some policies have benefit restoration periods that depend on being able to go a certain amount of time without using the policy (i.e., a 5-year benefit period is reinstated if a patient is in a nursing home and goes home for six months at the end of four years and no claims are filed for the six-month period). The practicality of this feature is questionable as the policyholder must depend on someone else to provide care during the required period out of the nursing home.

Most restoration provisions, however, require that the patient be really better, i.e., that no care is needed for a six-month period, or at least that no expenses that would be eligible under the policy be incurred for six months. A benefit like this is good for people who have short-term problems, like mild strokes, and fully recover. Someone who needs care for an extended period of time and is unlikely to get better will not benefit as much.

I was enjoying a lovely dinner at the annual board meeting of the university I attended until the gentleman on my right asked me to divulge my line of work. He recoiled when he heard the words "long-term care insurance" fall from my lips. I was soon to find out why. His wife was just coming up on her fourth year in a nursing home with Alzheimer's disease. Simultaneously, the benefits of her long-term care insurance were coming to an end. The agent who sold the policy had told him a four-year benefit period would be enough, because the policy had this great restoration feature and if she used up the four years, she could get her benefits restored. Since she will never recover, this has turned out to be very bad advice.

Some policies have separate benefit periods for home care, i.e. you could have five years for nursing home care and five years for home care, for a total of 10 years of coverage. If either side is used up, however, you can't tap into the other side to continue the benefits in the same location. In this example, if you use up the five years of home care benefits, and you still want to stay home, your remaining benefits will only be paid if you move to a nursing home.

Because of this problem, most policies today have "integrated" benefit periods. "Integrated" means that if you buy a six-year benefit period, for example, benefits will be paid however you need them—at home, in assisted living, adult day care, or in a nursing home.

Joint Policies

A new feature is catching on to make long-term care insurance policies more practical and affordable for married couples. Three versions of this idea exist in current policy selections:

1) One version allows spouses to share a benefit period at a lower premium than two separate benefit periods would cost. (You and the insurance company are betting that both spouses won't need a lot of long-term care.) If one spouse dies without using all the benefits, the surviving spouse is entitled to the remainder of the benefit period at a reduced premium.

2) Another version has separate benefit periods, but for a little more premium it allows spouses to access each other's benefit period. For example, each spouse has a six-year benefit period. If one spouse uses only one year of benefits then passes away, the other spouse would have eleven years of benefits left.

3) A third version provides separate benefit periods of the same length for each spouse, then allows the couple to purchase an additional benefit equal to the primary benefit period to share first come, first served. For example, if the spouses each purchased a three-year benefit period, the insurance company would allow them to purchase a third three-year benefit period that both could access as needed.

Elimination Period (Waiting Period)

This is the number of days that you have to pay until the insurance company pays benefits (like a deductible). Examples of choices range from 0, 20, 30, 60, 90, 100, 180, 365 or even 730 days. Some states won't allow waiting periods longer than 180 or even 100 days to be offered. Patients receiving skilled care may be able to avoid out-of-pocket costs during the elimination period because regular health insurance may pay some skilled care for people under 65 and Medicare can approve up to 100 days for skilled care for people over 65. The chances of qualifying for skilled care as long as 100 days are slim, however. (See *Why Doesn't Medicare Pay More?* on p. 15.)

The longer the elimination period, the greater the potential out-of-pocket costs. For example, someone with a 100-day waiting period who receives 30 days of skilled care reimbursed by private health insurance or Medicare, will be responsible for the 70 days of non-skilled care before the policy begins to pay. At a $140 charge per day, the out-of-pocket cost would be $9,800.

Caution: A few policies don't count days paid by Medicare or health insurance toward your waiting period. If you have a policy like the above example, you will be responsible for the full 100 days after the 30 days paid by Medicare. Ask the insurance agent to show you the section that addresses this point in the sample policy so you will have a clear understanding of how it works.

Some policies require the satisfaction of additional elimination periods if episodes of care are separated by longer than a specified time period, usually six months. For example, a patient may have a four-month nursing home stay and need to be admitted again four years later. Both admissions would require an elimination period before benefits could be paid. Most new policies require only one elimination period in a lifetime, regardless of how long it takes for you to accumulate the days of care that equal the waiting period. However, a few policies require you to accumulate the days within a certain time frame, such as six months or two years, in order for you to never have to satisfy another waiting period.

It is wise to ask how the elimination period is calculated for home health/adult day care. Some policies count only the days actual services are provided, so if the patient does not have home health care every day, it would take longer than 100 calendar days to satisfy a 100-day elimination period. Some policies count all seven days in a week toward the waiting period even though home care was only received on one day of that week. Others start counting when the physician first certifies the need for long-term care (see *Claims*' on p. 75). Policies of the latter type may not require charges to be incurred during the elimination period. In other words, family members could provide the care until the elimination period is satisfied.

Beware of policies that have choices of only 0 or 100 days, with no choice in between, especially if the agent is urging you to choose a 0-day waiting period, which means first day coverage and no deductible. This sounds great on the surface, but if that insurance company sells most of its policies without a deductible, it will most likely be paying out claims much faster than other insurance companies. Again, this sounds good, but it means the company will be much more apt to need rate increases to stay in business than other companies.

Mental Conditions

If you qualify for a policy, most policies will cover mental conditions only of an organic nature, such as Alzheimer's and other dementias. Look for a written statement about coverage for "cognitive impairment," which includes Alzheimer's disease. Most policies will not cover mental conditions of a non-organic nature such as schizophrenia, manic-depressive disorders, etc. People with "situational depression," e.g., due to loss of a spouse, usually can get a policy if their health is otherwise good. The new tax-qualified policies will cover severe cognitive impairment that causes the patient to be a threat to himself or others. For example, if you have high blood pressure and you can't remember to take your medicine when you are supposed to, this could certainly make you a threat to yourself. A few new policies cover all types of mental conditions.

Waiver of Premium

In most policies, premiums are waived after a specified time, usually expressed in days of benefit payments. For example, a typical policy will waive premiums after 90 days of nursing home benefits. Some policies do not require these days to be consecutive. Many policies also waive premiums when you receive assisted living, home care or adult day care, and some policies waive premiums on the first day of benefits. The premium only comes back in most policies, if you get truly better, which means you don't incur any eligible expenses, for six months.

Inflation Protection

The policy should have some provision to help the benefits keep pace with inflation because nursing home costs are projected to grow 5.8% compounded each year according to the General Accounting Office.[10] Here are two common inflation options offered by insurance companies:

Cost-of-Living (also called Future Purchase Option)

This method allows policyholders to buy extra coverage at certain intervals (i.e. every one to three years) equal to the percent of increase due to inflation. Typically, the amount of coverage offered is determined by changes in the Consumer Price Index and is offered as long as you haven't filed a claim in a certain period of time. Some states and some policies require those offers to continue even if you have had a claim. Some policies discontinue the offers if you turn them down four times, or even one time.

The problems with this method of inflation protection are:

1) The amount of the offer is usually determined by the overall Consumer Price Index, which is lower than the medical component of the CPI, neither of which are keeping up with actual increases in long-term care costs. Overall CPI in 2000 was 2.5% for all items and medical CPI was 4%. A few policies offer a minimum 5% annual offer.

2) The offers are priced at your attained age, which means the age you are when you accept each offer, not the age you were when you purchased the policy.

Guaranteed Annual Increases

Other policies allow the policyholder to purchase a rider that automatically increases the daily benefit by 5%—compounded or simple—for life. Most policies annually increase only the benefit, not the premium.

Proponents of the cost-of-living method argue that since medical costs can increase faster than 5% per year, policyholders with the inflation rider may experience a shortfall at the time of a claim, which would result in increased out-of-pocket costs. However, when the cost-of-living offers are determined by the overall Consumer Price Index, these offers are even more inadequate. People who like the 5% guaranteed annual increases method best say that the periodic premium increases under the cost-of-living method are unmanageable for most budgets, and the extra benefit usually can't be purchased if there is a claim. Someone who has a five year claim has a frozen daily benefit throughout the claim. (As noted above, some states and some policies require the future purchase offers to be made during a claim.) The 5% automatic annual increases occur even if there is a claim, and—a pleasant surprise—the premium is usually waived. (See *Waiver of Premium,* p. 54.)

The biggest problem with the cost-of-living method is that it has a lower premium when the policy is first purchased, but over the long run can cost much more than purchasing the rider that guarantees a 5% automatic annual increase. For example, a 54-year old starting out with an annual premium of $869 could be paying $31,380 per year by age 87 if she accepted offers equal to 5% compounded, or a total of $206,598 in premium over those 33 years. By comparison, she could have purchased the policy with a rider that increases the benefit 5% compounded each year for the rest of her life at an annual premium of $1,764. By age 87, she would only have paid $58,212 in premium over the 33 year period vs. $206,598 with the cost-of-living method!

If you are considering the future purchase offer method, be sure and ask the insurance agent to show you a printout of the projected premium increases over your lifetime. The insurance companies who offer this method of inflation protection are required to include that information in the proposal.

If you elect the 5% rider instead of the cost-of-living method, you may be wondering if you should choose the 5% simple (if your state allows that option) or the 5% compounded rate of growth. "Simple" means the benefit grows 5% of the original amount and doubles in 20 years. "Compounded" increases grow faster, doubling in 15 years, because the 5% increase is based on the previous year. Walter Newman, a North Carolina insurance agent, tells how this benefit really paid off at claim time:

In 1992, a locally prominent man bought a policy from me with a $100 daily benefit. After some persuasion, he agreed to add the 5-percent compound inflation rider. He was a wealthy individual and wanted to buy a plan without inflation coverage, intending to self-insure the difference.

Three years later he was diagnosed with Alzheimer's and was cared for at home for the next two years. When his family could no longer manage him, he was admitted to a skilled nursing facility. Thanks to the inflation coverage, he is currently receiving benefits of $141 per day, instead of the original benefit of $100 per day. The cost of his care is $5,500 a month, leaving a difference of $1,138. His family tells me his Social Security check just about makes up the difference, so all his other income and assets are available to his family. If he hadn't bought the inflation rider, the difference would have been almost $2,500!

Obviously, the younger the applicant, the better sense the 5% compounded makes, since long-term care costs are projected to triple in the next 20 years.[11] Anyone 70 and younger is well advised to consider the 5% compounded inflation method because people are living so long today. People in their 70's may want to choose 5% simple to get a lower premium. The example on the next page shows that the growth for the first 10 years is very close to the 5% compounded rate.

Another way people, age 75 or older can protect against inflation is to buy a higher benefit than the average cost of care (i.e. $200+ per day at age 78, or $350+ per day for high cost areas like New York, Massachusetts, Alaska, etc.) to build in extra benefit to accommodate future costs.

It's the old "pay now or pay later" problem if you are thinking about not buying inflation coverage because it increases the premium so much. You can wind up on welfare immediately if your benefit is far below the cost of care when you have a claim and you can't make up the difference out of your pocket. Look at the example on page 60 before making your decision.

Rates vs. Ratings

Virtually all policies today lock in the rate at the time of purchase based on the age of the applicant and cannot increase premiums unless all policyholders in a certain class receive the same increase. Very few policies are "noncancellable," which means the premium can never increase. Some states will not approve a noncancellable policy because higher than anticipated demand for long-term care benefits could make it difficult for an insur-

The following chart shows a comparison of a $100 daily benefit with a 5% simple growth vs. a 5% compounded growth.

Year	5% Simple	5% Compounded
1	$100.00	$100.00
2	105.00	105.00
3	110.00	110.00
4	115.00	116.00
5	120.00	122.00
6	125.00	128.00
7	130.00	134.00
8	135.00	141.00
9	140.00	148.00
10	145.00	155.00
11	150.00	163.00
12	155.00	171.00
13	160.00	180.00
14	165.00	189.00
15	170.00	198.00
16	175.00	208.00
17	180.00	218.00
18	185.00	229.00
19	190.00	241.00
20	195.00	253.00
21	200.00	265.00
22	205.00	279.00
23	210.00	293.00
24	215.00	307.00
25	220.00	323.00
26	225.00	339.00
27	230.00	356.00
28	235.00	373.00
29	240.00	392.00
30	245.00	412.00
31	250.00	432.00

Pay Now or Pay Later

Age: 65, married
Daily Benefit: $150
Waiting Period: 20 days
Benefit Period: Lifetime (Unlimited)
Home Health: Same benefits as nursing home

Client #1: Daily benefit grows 5% compounded annually for life

Client #2: Either no inflation or policy has future purchase offers, but client doesn't purchase future amounts

Annual Premium: $4,286.52 x 20 years = **$85,730**

Annual Premium: $2,313.36 x 20 years = **$46,267**

ASSUMPTION: Client #2 has a long-term care need in 20 years at age 85. Daily cost in 20 years: **$450/day* or $165,000**

Client #2's deficit = $300 per day ($450 cost –$150 daily benefit purchased) X 365 days = $109,500 shortfall first year. (Shortfall grows each year as cost continues to grow with inflation.)

Client #2 "saved" $39,463 in premium over the twenty-year period, but applying the savings to the first year shortfall still leaves $70,037 coming out of Client #2's pocket and $109,500+ for years two and forward.

QUESTION: Did Client #2 Really Save?

*Annual growth rate of 5.8% according to the General Accounting Office, 6/91 and the Health Care Financing Administration, 7/99.

ance company to hold the rate. Initial pricing and the type of underwriting, liberal or conservative, will play major roles in an insurance company's rate stability. "Underwriting" refers to the type of health conditions that an insurance company will accept when a person applies for coverage. Below-market rates, liberal underwriting (i.e., accepting a lot of people with major health problems), and a small asset base make future rate increases almost a certainty.

Do not even think of shopping for the cheapest long-term care insurance policy you can find. Some companies that started out with extremely low premium (i.e., half to two-thirds of other companies' rates) have already experienced terrific rate increases, whereas most companies have not experienced a rate increase for policies issued in the past decade, if ever. If a company is having rate increases now, what will happen to it when the baby boomers begin needing long-term care? This point can't be overemphasized. There have been cases of premiums not just doubling, but increasing 800%! If the premium is significantly less than other policies, run, don't walk, away from it.

Some legitimate premium savings can be had by paying annual premium vs. a monthly bankdraft. A few policies don't charge extra or may even reward you with a small discount for bankdraft, but annual premium is the least expensive payment with most companies. Loads of 9% for monthly and 5.5% for semi-annual are common. Rather than pay the load, many people pay annual premium out of their investments. A common strategy to find the money to pay a long-term care premium without taking it out of monthly living expenses is to convert a low-interest bearing fund such as a CD or money market account to a deferred annuity that will earn a higher interest rate tax-deferred. Most annuities allow you to withdraw 10% or so annually with no penalty or surrender charge and that makes a great funding vehicle for the annual long-term care premium. Check with your accountant when you are setting up the amount to ensure that the withdrawals accommodate your tax needs as well as the long-term care policy premium.

Married people get a break with spouse discounts ranging from as low as 7.5% to as high as 10-25%. Some companies even give the discount if one spouse is declined for coverage due to a health problem or just doesn't apply for coverage in the first place. The insurance companies are betting that most married people will try to take care of each other as long as possible and not use as many claims dollars as single people without the live-in support system of a spouse.

Some of the spouse discounts extend to live-in siblings and a few are really a household discount that could include anyone living with you in a long-term situation. There are even policies that grant a 50% discount, but don't get fooled by the size of the discount. Compare in real dollars to decide if the premium is either too low or too high.

A few policies allow you to pay two years' annual premium when you purchase the policy in exchange for a lower lifetime rate; e.g. a 25% discount for the second year forward.

In addition to avoiding bargain basement premiums, it is not wise to consider a carrier with less than an A- rating by A. M. Best, the most well-known third-party rating service for insurance companies. Carriers with lower ratings may not have the financial strength to sustain long-term care coverage. It is also

Financial Quality Ratings of Major Rating Agencies

DESCRIPTION OF RATING	STANDARD AND POOR'S	MOODY'S	A. M. BEST	FITCH
SUPERIOR	AAA	Aaa	A++ A+	AAA
EXCELLENT	AA+ AA AA-	Aa1 Aa2 Aa3	A A-	AA+ AA AA-
VERY GOOD			B++ B+	
GOOD	A+ A A-	A1 A2 A3	B B-	A+ A A-
ADEQUATE	BBB+ BBB BBB-	Baa1 Baa2 Baa3		BBB+ BBB BBB-
FAIR			C++ C+	
BELOW AVERAGE	BB+ BB BB-	Ba1 Ba2 Ba3		BB+ BB BB-
MARGINAL			C C-	
FINANCIALLY WEAK	B+ B B-	B1 B2 B3		B+ B B-
HIGHLY VULNERABLE OR NONVIABLE	CCC CC C	Caa Ca C		
BELOW MINIMUM STANDARDS			D	
UNDER STATE SUPERVISION			E	
IN LIQUIDATION			F	

wise to ask if the carrier has assets in the billions, or if it is owned or reinsured by a company with assets that large.

"Reinsured" means that a larger company will pay claims after they reach a certain size. Some smaller companies are subsidiaries of "billion" -dollar companies; however, subsidiaries can always be sold. A major reason insurance companies have withdrawn from the long-term care insurance market is because they could not keep up with product design required by regulatory changes. Many smaller companies just don't have the financial flexibility to make these changes in a timely manner necessary to be competitive in the market. The chart on the previous page may help you examine ratings of companies. This gives an outline of the rating scales used by the four primary rating services. To get ratings on selected companies over the telephone at no cost, you can call Standard & Poor's at 212-438-2000, Moody's at 212-553-0377, and Fitch (formerly Duff & Phelps) at 800-853-4824. The A. M. Best rating can be obtained by visiting the reference section of your local library. Ask for the most recent Best's book, because it is published annually. Ratings are updated more frequently in the monthly magazine, *Best's Review.*

Rates (premiums) are the same for men and women, but are based on age. Policies are available for ages 18+, but most are sold in the 40-84 range. You're never too young to think about long-term care insurance—a 25-year-old can wind up in a coma after a car accident! If you haven't bought a policy by the time you are 40, pre-retirement ages (40's and 50's) are the best time to consider long-term care coverage, because premiums are lower and health is better at younger ages. (A few policies have a single pay option or allow you to stop paying after either 10 or 20 years or at age 65.)

The True Cost of Waiting

There are three solid reasons why you should ignore advice to wait until you are in your 50's or 60's to purchase a long-term care policy.

1. Anything could happen to you—see examples of younger people needing long-term care in *Long-Term Care Insurance is Not "Senior Citizen Insurance,"* on p. 113.

2. Because of Point #1, you may not be insurable. No amount of money will buy you a long-term care insurance policy after you develop a serious health condition.

Kathy Halverson's 41-year-old husband was diagnosed in 1986 with Parkinson's disease. An insurance agent in Wisconsin, he and Kathy "had it all" when it came to insurance policies—except long-term care insurance. Kathy had to learn the insurance business and take over his practice to care for him and provide for their family, especially their children's education. Her husband has since passed away, and Kathy has dedicated herself to getting the word out about how long-term care insurance can protect families. She repeatedly testifies, "We sold insurance for 31 years! We had it all . . . but not LTC . . . and after spending all our pensions, retirement, etc., to care for my husband and educate our children, we were 10 months away from seeking assistance [with Medicaid]."

3. You will pay longer, but you will pay less. The longer you wait, the more benefit you must purchase because long-term care costs are increasing so rapidly. Consider that a 30-year-old may wish to purchase a policy that

will pay about 2/3 of the cost. Today he could consider a $90 daily benefit for a premium of $440. If that person waited until 40 to purchase, he would have to buy a $150 daily benefit for a premium of $733 to accomplish his goal because the cost of care in 10 years will be about $220. At 50 years old, he is looking at a $250 daily benefit to pay 2/3 of the cost, for a premium of $1,682. Now multiply all three premium amounts to age 80 to see how much he would pay, depending on his purchase age. ($440 x 50 years = $22,000 vs. $733 x 40 years = $29,320 vs. $1,682 x 30 years = $50,460)

The difference is most dramatic from age 40 to age 50, but both of those ages become a moot point if he has a skiing accident at age 35 and becomes paralyzed for the rest of his life.

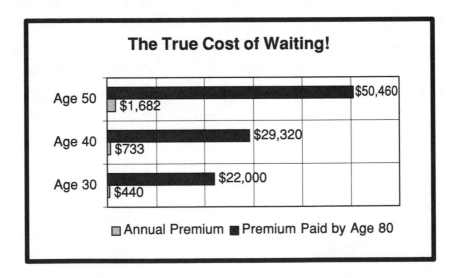

Consumer advocates advising you to wait until you're older to buy may change their advice when a younger sister or son is paralyzed from a car accident or rendered almost lifeless from a stroke or aneurysm.

Saving vs. LTC Insurance

Consider the following example of purchasing a long-term care policy versus investing in an IRA to fund long-term care. A man or woman invests $250 in an IRA at age 40 (after an initial investment of $500 to open the IRA). He or she continues to put $250 annually in the IRA until age 70½, which is the mandatory IRA distribution age. That consumer will have $26,519 ($250 each year compounded annually at 6½ percent). While that sounds like a tidy sum for a minimum investment, it will barely pay for six months of long-term care at today's cost of over $50,000, much less the projected cost of $275,000 per year in 30 years. Suppose the man or woman had decided to purchase long-term care insurance at age 40. For a little more than twice this $250 IRA investment, he or she can get coverage of $90 per day* for all benefits (home care, assisted living, adult day care and nursing home care) with a total benefit period of four years and a waiting period of only 60 days. Since this plan includes a 5% compounded inflation feature, in 40 years at age 80 the daily benefit will grow to $610 per day. The annual married premium is only $659 per spouse. If the insured does not have a claim until age 80, he or she will have paid about $27,000 in premiums, and the total available benefit payout will have grown to a whopping $890,600 or about $1.7 million for both spouses. And, don't forget that the premium stops when you are using the policy!

On the other end of the age spectrum, a 70-year-old couple may decide to save $6,950 a year, instead of spending that amount to pay the premium for a rich plan with a $150 daily benefit that will fully cover today's cost. (The other elements are the same as

*A good plan that pays about two-thirds of the cost in most parts of the country.

the plan described above for the 40-year-old.) By age 80, the couple will have saved $121,842 at 10% before taxes and investment fees, which sounds like a lot until you realize that the cost of care at that time is projected to be $89,060. Their savings at age 80 would pay for less than 1½ years of care for only one person. Had the couple bought the long-term care insurance policies, the $150 daily benefit would have grown to $234 per day by age 80, and the couple would have had an available benefit of $85,410 a year for each of them, and a potential payout of $683,240 for a four year benefit period for two people.

Underwriting

Applicants for individual policies must qualify medically for long-term care coverage. Progressive conditions such as Alzheimer's, Parkinson's disease, AIDS, multiple sclerosis, muscular dystrophy, and psychiatric disorders are uninsurable. Applicants must be ambulatory to qualify for coverage, and must not need help with activities of daily living, such as bathing, dressing, toileting, transferring from bed to chair, eating or continence. Heart disease, cancer or one mild stroke can be acceptable risks after recovery periods of usually between two and five years, depending on the insurance company. Conditions such as hypertension are acceptable if controlled. Diabetes (contracted later in life, not during childhood) can be insurable if it is well under control, especially non-insulin dependent. Some companies will accept up to 50 units of insulin per day. People who take antidepressants for "situational depression" (death of a spouse, for example) usually can get a policy if their health otherwise is good.

The standard basis for underwriting is medical records from your doctor, instead of a physical exam, although some insurance companies are utilizing paramedical or face-to-face exams. A paramedical exam means a home health nurse visits you to check your blood pressure, height, weight, and to do a quick assessment of your overall physical and mental health. Some companies require a blood test for younger applicants to check for HIV. A "face-to-face" exam means that someone personally interviews you to be sure you are in good mental health. Many companies require this for applicants ages 75 and up. Underwriting commonly includes a telephone interview.

Caution: A carrier with "loose" underwriting may need future rate increases sooner than a carrier with conservative underwriting. Also, there are horror stories about carriers who do "post-claim underwriting" (i.e. medical history is thoroughly investigated **after** a claim is filed, which naturally results in a large number of denied claims.) This practice is illegal today, but be wary of a "yes/no" application with a policy issued to you in a very short period of time. It usually takes about 4–6 weeks for a policy to be issued, because the company is doing a good job of checking your mental and physical health to see if you qualify for coverage.

Some carriers will accept health problems if you pay a higher premium or will make alternative benefit offers. For example, you may be offered a four- or five-year benefit period instead of an unlimited benefit period, or a 90- or 100-day waiting period instead of a 20- or 60-day elimination period.

The most important thing about underwriting is that the younger you are, the better the chance you have to qualify for a policy. **No amount of money will purchase long-term care**

**insurance for you once you are uninsurable due to a signifi-
cant physical or mental health problem.** People are strongly
encouraged to apply for long-term care insurance certainly by
the time they reach their 40's and 50's (pre-retirement ages).
Of course, premiums are lower at younger ages and are locked
in at the younger age unless there is a rate increase for an entire
classification of policyholders.

Pre-Existing Conditions

An ideal policy will cover the policyholder from the effective
date of the policy for all conditions disclosed on the application.
Many policies have no restrictions at all for pre-existing conditions. A few policies have a 90- to 180-day waiting period for
pre-existing conditions.

"Free-Look" Period

Policies issued today must contain a thirty-day period after policy delivery in which the policyholder may return the policy for
a full return of premium if not satisfied for any reason.

Non-Forfeiture Options

For additional premium, some policies (more commonly non-
tax qualified policies) may guarantee to return a specified percentage of premium to a beneficiary if the policy was not used
after being in force a specified number of years. For example, a
policy may guarantee to return a scheduled percentage of the
premium if the policyholder terminates the policy or dies after
the policy has been held at least five years. Some policies return
all of the premiums if the policy is held at least 20 or more years.

This feature usually costs about 30% or more in premium. The odds of using the policy and getting nothing back are very high, especially if you purchased home health care benefits. However, for even more premium, a few policies will return 100% of the premium to you, or your estate if you are deceased, after a specified number of years even if you have used the policy.

A partial daily or monthly benefit may stay in effect if the policyholder stops paying premium after five years or so. Known as a "reduced paid-up benefit," this feature has not been popular. Because the benefit is so potentially small at claim time, the policyholder is at risk to make up large balances from the very first day of care.

The policyholder must decide if these "money-back" features are worth the additional premium, or if a greater return on investment can be achieved by putting the difference in premium in a mutual fund or other type of growth investment, such as annuities, individual stocks and bonds, or life insurance, which is frequently used in wealth preservation and estate tax planning strategies.

A few tax-qualified policies have a cash-back nonforfeiture benefit but any refunded premium that was used for a tax deduction creates a taxable event upon its return.

More commonly, tax-qualified policies contain an option for a nonforfeiture benefit called a "shortened benefit period." You are not required to purchase it. If you do purchase it, the "value" will not be cash back as described above. Instead, the tax-qualified version of nonforfeiture guarantees that if you terminate your policy after three years in most states (after ten years in

California), the insurance company must pay benefits equal to the amount of premium you have paid for any claim you have in the future, even though your policy is no longer in force.

For example, you paid $15,000 in premium and then decided to cancel your policy. If you had purchased this feature and you had a claim the day after you cancelled your policy, the insurance company would have to pay benefits at the daily benefit in force on the day you cancelled your policy up to $15,000. If your daily benefit were $100, the company would pay 150 days of benefits, or five months. If you had a claim 10 or 15 years from now, the company would still pay benefits of $100 per day up to $15,000. However, at future prices, this would probably pay for only a few weeks of care. This feature will cost you about 30% more in premium with most policies.

A few companies will give you the "shortened benefit period" nonforfeiture benefit, even though you didn't pay extra for it if your premium goes up past a certain predetermined point based on the age you were when you purchased the policy. For example, if you purchased your policy at age 60, the predetermined point might be 70%. So if you had a rate increase that took your premium to 71% more than your original premium, the insurance company would have to give you the "shortened benefit period" nonforfeiture benefit.

This is called "contingent nonforfeiture," because your receiving the benefit is contingent upon your premium being raised to the predetermined point that triggers the benefit. This means you could stop paying your premium and the insurance company would have to pay a claim for you at any point in the future equal to the premium you had paid in. Or, if you wanted to keep your policy in force without the additional rate increase, you could do so by accepting a reduced benefit offer that the insurance company is required to extend to you. Your benefit would be lowered, but you could keep the same premium and you would not have to pay the additional rate increase.

The National Association of Insurance Commissioners is working to require all insurance companies to provide contingent nonforfeiture, because they believe it will act as a deterrent to unnecessary rate increases. Since companies don't want to give this benefit away without the additional premium it normally costs, this requirement serves as an incentive for the insurance companies to do everything possible to hold your premium down so it won't increase to the point that makes the company give you the "shortened benefit period" nonforfeiture benefit free.

If your budget forces you to choose between nonforfeiture and inflation coverage, buy inflation coverage.

Assets

Individuals without assets outside a home and/or car are usually not candidates for long-term care insurance as they will quickly qualify for Medicaid. The National Association of Insurance Commissioners believes you may not be a candidate for long-term care insurance if you have an income less than $20,000 and/or assets less than $30,000, not counting your house and car. The exception to this thinking occurs when a family member (such as a child for a parent) purchases a policy to provide a higher level of care than that offered by Medicaid reimbursement and to ensure an option for home health care and other community choices such as assisted living or adult day care. Or, if nursing home care is needed as a last resort, the adult son or daughter wants the parent to have a complete choice of nursing homes. Many nursing homes have waiting lists and many admit only private-pay patients or patients with long-term care insurance as both types of patients can pay higher rates than the Medicaid reimbursement level. Since a number of nursing homes no longer accept Medicaid patients, people trying to enter a nursing home as a Medicaid patient sometimes have to go to a facility several hours away from the desired location.

Because of the poor choices on Medicaid, another exception to this rule occurs when people who are "house rich and cash poor" obtain a reverse mortgage on their home and use some of that money to purchase long-term care insurance to avoid being on Medicaid.

Some people with assets of $500,000 or more consider paying for their own long-term care. Sometimes the question is: How much of your asset base is liquid? Or will a long-term care need force you to sell property and/or investments at a loss because of poor market timing? **If you have less than $2 million in assets, it is very risky to try to self-insure your long-term care expenses.** Many financial planners advise clients with less than $5 million in assets to purchase LTC insurance.

Another reason people with significant assets buy long-term care insurance is to avoid confrontations with children over how much money is spent for long-term care. Others will purchase long-term care insurance to preserve privacy of financial records. Without a policy, private-pay nursing home patients usually have to show financial records to prove long-term payment capability. Finally, people with significant assets sometimes purchase long-term care insurance because they want money that would be spent on long-term care to go to other causes such as charities, church, their university alumni association or, their grandchildren, like the gentleman who owned several McDonald's in *The Private Sector Solution* in Chapter One.

Claims

Prior to the tax-qualified policies that were introduced 1/1/97, most policies required your doctor to tell the insurance company that you needed help with at least two Activities of Daily Living (ADLs) before a claim could be paid, although a few policies only required help with one ADL. These are generally dressing, eating, transferring from bed to chair, toileting and maintaining continence. Some policies include bathing in the list. These policies have the potential to pay sooner, as bathing is usually the first ADL that people need help with. Two states added a seventh ADL to the list: Texas required "mobility" and California required "ambulating"—both just a measurement of being able to move around well. Help with ADLs can be "hands on," which means direct physical contact, but better policies also allow "stand-by" or supervisory assistance from the person who is helping you.

If you can physically perform the Activities of Daily Living but have to be told when and how to do them because you have a "cognitive impairment," the better policies issued prior to 1/1/97 will still pay your claim. Cognitive impairment is usually determined by a standardized test to determine deficiencies such as short-or long-term memory loss and general orientation (knowing one's name, place of residence, current political leaders, date, time, etc.) or bizarre hygiene habits.

The new tax-qualified policies sold after 1/1/97 changed the requirements somewhat to get a claim paid. Tax-qualified policies will pay a claim if you are expected to need help for at least 90 days with 2 or more of at least 5 Activities of Daily Living from this list:

bathing	dressing
toileting	transferring
eating	continence

This means that insurance companies can use a list of five or six ADLs, which means some companies will include bathing in their list and some won't. Some will include bathing and omit one of the other ADLs, most commonly continence. California requires insurance companies to use all six ADLs. The 90-day certification must be provided by a licensed health care practitioner (physician, registered nurse or licensed social worker). **The 90-day certification is not a waiting period.** If you have a 20-day waiting period, for example, your policy will begin paying benefits on the 21st day you need care as long as your doctor (or nurse or social worker) says that you are expected to need help with at least 2 ADLs for longer than 90 days.

The 90-day certification just assures that long-term care insurance will be preserved to pay for truly long-term conditions. Short-term conditions like fractures and mild strokes usually require skilled care such as physical, speech or occupational therapy. The previous sections *Why Doesn't Private Insurance Pay More?* on p. 14 and *Why Doesn't Medicare Pay More?* on p. 15, explain that conventional health insurance and Medicare pay only for skilled care and will therefore cover most short-term conditions, also called "sub-acute" or "post-acute" care.

The new policies also pay if you can do all of the Activities of Daily Living, but you need help due to a severe cognitive impairment. This means that you are cognitively impaired to the point of being a threat to yourself or others. For example, if you can't remember how to take your medicine appropriately and you have high blood pressure, you are probably a threat to yourself since by not taking your medicine when you are supposed to could cause you to have a stroke.

Non-tax-qualified policies are still being offered by some insurance companies, and the state of California even requires them to be offered to California policyholders. These policies do not require the 90-day certification, and may require help with only one Activity of Daily Living to get a claim paid. Instead of needing help with Activities of Daily Living or being cognitively impaired, some non-tax-qualified policies will also pay a claim if your doctor says you need care that is "medically necessary," which means that you need care for some type of illness or injury. Most policies like this allow only nursing home benefits to be paid if you need medically necessary care, but a few policies will allow home care to be paid as well. For example, you may be able to perform all of the Activities of Daily Living and you may not be cognitively impaired, but you can't completely take care of yourself because you have crippling arthritis in your back. If your policy pays "homemaker" benefits such as cooking, cleaning, laundry, etc., and pays for medically necessary care under the home health benefit, it could pay for homemaker services because your arthritis makes it medically necessary for you to have help. This "medically necessary" benefit trigger is not in the new tax-qualified policies.

Needing help with Activities of Daily Living, cognitive impairment or needing help because it's medically necessary are all called "benefit triggers," because satisfying one of these requirements is necessary to get the policy to pay benefits.

Tax-Qualified or Non-Tax Qualified

Some people say that the new tax-qualified policies are more restrictive than policies sold before 1/1/97 because of the required 90-day certification and because the medically necessary benefit trigger is no longer allowed. While this is true, there is a very good reason for the tightening up of the access to benefits.

A few years before this law was passed, long-term care policies began growing more liberal. Some policies would pay for any type of care at home or in a nursing home if help was needed with only one Activity of Daily Living, and the list included bathing. A growing number of policies also had the medical necessity benefit trigger. That made it easier to collect benefits, especially when it applied to home health care. A couple of policies were introduced that would pay nursing home care at the "policyholder's discretion"—that means you say you want to go to a nursing home and the insurance company pays your claim! Another policy that became extremely popular paid benefits if you just needed help with two "Instrumental Activities of Daily Living," such as cooking, cleaning, laundry, grocery shopping, telephoning for doctor's appointments, and the like. This brings to mind the old phrase, "If it sounds too good to be true, it usually is."

Why did this happen? The free enterprise system allows insurance companies the opportunity to sell more policies by offering policies with liberal benefit access. The combination of easy access to benefits, low premiums and liberal underwriting (which means that policies are issued commonly to people with significant health problems) means these companies could be more competitive in the marketplace and sell more policies. But these features that sound so good now mean bad news for the consumer in the long run in the form of future rate increases.

Congress saw this trend and stepped in. If the benefits are too easy to obtain, and if the policies are sold to people who have a high likelihood of using the coverage in a short period of time, the policies will pay out more than the collected premiums will support. This means that in the next 10–15 years when the claims activity is high, the long-term care insurance market could "crash" due to large rate increases that many consumers could not afford to pay. And, of course, smaller insurance companies can be hit harder and need bigger rate increases than larger, more financially solvent companies, and that's if they are even able to stay in business.

The taxation issue often is presented as the center of the controversy on whether to purchase a tax-qualified or non-tax qualified policy, i.e., will the IRS ever rule that benefits from a non-tax-qualified policy are taxable income?

Insurance companies are required to provide Form 1099-LTC to anyone who receives benefits from any type of long-term care insurance policy, tax-qualified or non-tax-qualified. The policyholder is required to report benefits paid from any type of long-term care insurance policy to the IRS on Form 8853, Medical Savings Accounts and Long-Term Care Insurance Contracts. The IRS matches up these 1099s with individual tax filings and sends letters requesting an explanation from people who failed to report benefits received from long-term care insurance policies.

Some insurance companies that actively promote non-tax-qualified policies promise to convert your policy to a tax-qualified policy if the IRS makes such a ruling. Read the fine print. The state of California requires such an exchange *unless the policyholder is already receiving benefits.* In that situation, the policyholder would be stuck receiving benefits that are 100% taxable income! Beware of advisors who explain nonchalantly that it's no big deal because the cost of your care is a deductible medical expense that will offset the taxable income. Not so! IRS Form 1040: Schedule A—Itemized Deductions plainly states in the block marked "Medical and Dental Expenses": *Caution: Do not include expenses reimbursed or paid by others.* Any amount reimbursed by a non-tax-qualified policy cannot be deducted as a medical expense.

Is the tax question the real issue or was Congress trying to use the tax liability as a velvet hammer to swing the market to tax-qualified policies with more reasonable benefit triggers?

The measures Congress took in the 1996 health care reform legislation will function as *consumer protection measures* to ensure that long-term care insurance is there for us when we need it by restoring long-term care insurance to its original purpose, and that is to pay for long-term conditions.

Getting a Claim Paid

Regardless of which type of policy you buy, the better insurance companies have streamlined claims filing procedures. Most allow you to call an 800 number and notify the company that the need for long-term care has arisen. At that point the claims representative will assist you with the necessary paperwork and help you obtain the 90-day certification from the appropriate medical authority. Most companies will even pay for a care coordinator, which is someone to evaluate your needs on a local level to ensure that you get the appropriate level of care in the best setting for your condition, i.e., home care, adult day care, assisted living or nursing home care.

When claims are paid, the benefit checks are usually sent to you, but some insurance companies will pay the provider of care if you like, especially if the provider files the claim for you. If this is your choice, it's a good idea to get a family member or someone else you trust to audit the bills and claim payments every month to be sure you are being billed correctly for the services you receive.

Ask the insurance agent or company for references from satisfied policyholders who have been through the claims filing process. You can also ask the department of insurance in your state if any complaints have been filed about the insurance company. (See **Appendix B** for the address and telephone number of your state's insurance department.)

Miscellaneous Benefits

The better policies today have a variety of benefits in addition to those already described.

Alternate Plan of Care—If your doctor and the insurance company agree that you can be taken care of at home adequately, some policies allow money taken from your benefits to provide enhancements to your home, such as handrails, wheelchair ramps, shower stall improvements, etc., or even an emergency response system to make it easier for you to stay home. This benefit is also used to pay for new long-term care services as they are developed. This is a great feature, because without it, the insurance company would have to amend your policy to pay for new services, a process that can take a long time.

Caution: Beware of anyone who tells you the "alternate plan of care" benefit means it is not necessary to purchase home health coverage when you buy your policy. You may be able to get some home care assistance under the "alternate plan of care" provision, but it is by no means a defined benefit for home care, assisted living or adult day care. If you want home care benefits, make sure that the "home care" block is checked on the application, and that your policy specifically states that you have benefits for home care, assisted living and adult day care. (The real intent of the "alternate plan of care" provision is to find ways to provide care that is less expensive than nursing home care.)

Hospice—Most long-term care insurance policies cover hospice, which is care for terminally ill people to keep them as comfortable as possible and provide respite care to family members. Most health insurance policies also cover hospice and Medicare has a virtually unlimited benefit for hospice. Tax-qualified policies are not allowed to duplicate Medicare payments, so when would the long-term care policy pay? Medicare's inpatient respite care benefit for hospice is only five days per stay and the family may need a longer period of respite care. Medicare's home care benefit for hospice won't pay eight-hour shifts or longer except in a crisis situation. Long-term care insurance will pay eight-hour shifts indefinitely as long as benefit triggers are met and benefit maximums are not exhausted.

Respite Care—a specific benefit to give the primary caregiver a break. The break could be a few hours off to go shopping or a week or two for a vacation. This benefit is usually paid at home but the better policies pay also in a nursing home or assisted living facility to cover the 24-hour care that will be needed if the caregiver needs to be away several days. Benefit triggers (Activities of Daily Living or cognitive impairment) usually must be met to access the respite care benefit, but the elimination period normally does not have to be satisfied.

Homemaker Services—a benefit that pays for personal caregiving services such as cooking, cleaning, laundry, shopping, telephoning and transportation when a benefit trigger is met. Some policies will pay homemaker services only when you are receiving other home care services, such as care provided by a home health aide, nurse or therapist.

Alternate Payer Designation (Third Party Notification)—The policyholder designates someone else to get a copy of a lapse notice in case the policyholder doesn't pay the premium. This protects against policies lapsing because policyholders develop a mental or physical problem that makes them unable to pay the premium.

Impairment Reinstatement—If the policyholder allows the policy to lapse due to a cognitive or physical impairment, the insurance company will reinstate the policy with appropriate premium payment within a specific time period, such as five, six, or nine months. Without this provision in the policy, an insurance company is under no obligation to reinstate your policy if you miss the grace period by even one day. All tax-qualified policies have a minimum reinstatement period of five months.

Bed Reservation—If you have to go to a hospital during a nursing home stay, this benefit will pay to hold your bed at the nursing home. Without this benefit, your family would have to pay or the nursing home could give the bed to someone else. Since nursing homes are 88% full nationwide,[12] most nursing homes have waiting lists. Without a bed hold payment, you would have to find another nursing home if you lost your bed to someone else and the nursing home was full. Some policies provide the bed-reservation benefit when the patient leaves the nursing home to visit family and friends, and many policies also pay to hold your bed if you have to go to the hospital while you are in an assisted living facility.

Care Coordination—This benefit pays a third party who ideally doesn't work for the insurance company or the provider of care to manage your care and report regularly to your family, although some companies require you to use care coordinators affiliated with the insurance company or raise or lower the benefit level by whether or not you use the recommended care coordinator. The "care coordinator" would perform services like helping to determine the best place for you to receive care, i.e., at home, in an assisted living facility, adult day care or a nursing home and making sure you are getting the best care possible.

A care coordinator is especially helpful when children or other family members don't live nearby, because the care coordinator can give "care reports" regularly to the family members. Some companies want policyholders to use this benefit so much that they don't reduce the benefit maximum whenever you use it. They feel this way because they know a care coordinator will help you get the most out of your long-term care policy by using your benefits most effectively and efficiently. Some companies require the use of care coordinators before paying benefits at all.

Survivor Benefit—Some policies will not require a surviving spouse to pay premiums after the death of a spouse if the death occurs after the policy has been held a specified period of time, usually 10 years, but it could be less. For example, if the death occurs prior to the 10th year, the surviving spouse would only pay until the 10th policy anniversary.

Worldwide Coverage—Most long-term care policies will not pay outside the United States, but a few will pay worldwide, especially if you live in the U.S. at least six months of the year. Some policies pay in the U.S. and Canada.

Coordination with Medicare and Other Insurance—Tax-qualified policies are not allowed to make a payment if Medicare pays or if Medicare would pay in the absence of a deductible or coinsurance. Some companies interpret this provision in its strictest sense, i.e., if Medicare makes a payment on days 21-100 for nursing home care, the long-term care policy will not make a payment, even though you are responsible for a daily co-payment for those days. Most people, however, have coverage to supplement Medicare for the first 100 days—either a Medicare supplement, retiree plan or HMO. (This is further evidence that Congress intends long-term care insurance to pay for long-term conditions beyond three months, not short-term recovery conditions.)

A few policies coordinate with any other health insurance, which could include another long-term care policy but rarely does. Some companies police it another way: They won't sell you a daily or monthly benefit that, together with the policy you already have, would exceed the maximum daily or monthly benefit they offer.

Additional Benefits—Long-term care policies commonly include payment for a medical alert/emergency response system (usually $25-$50 a month), ambulance (4 trips per year) and medical equipment (30-50 times the daily benefit). Some of these expenses are picked up by Medicare and most policies will not duplicate Medicare's payment. These types of benefits are nice to have, but they shouldn't be given equal weight in the buying decision with the other benefits discussed in this chapter.

Policy Improvements

Ask your agent how the insurance company has treated existing policyholders when new policies or policy improvements to existing policies have been introduced. Were the existing policyholders offered the new policy or improvements for a period of time (90 days perhaps) without medical questions? Was premium charged at current age, or age when the policy was first purchased? The better companies don't treat existing policyholders like brand new applicants when new policies or policy improvements are offered.

Note: Policies purchased prior to 1991 may have benefit restrictions that need to be analyzed carefully to see if you need to upgrade or replace your policy with a new one. Some examples of restrictions in these older policies are:

▲ a "prior hospitalization" requirement before benefits for nursing home can be paid

▲ a "prior nursing home" requirement before benefits for home health care can be paid (if home care benefits are important to you)

▲ a requirement for skilled care before non-skilled care can be paid

▲ a lower benefit for non-skilled nursing home care than skilled care

▲ an exclusion for Alzheimer's disease and other organic mental disorders

▲ a 50% home health care benefit if care is required to be provided by a home health agency

▲ no inflation coverage

Caution: Upgrading a policy that was issued before 1/1/97 may cause you to lose the "grandfathered" status that allows it to be a tax-qualified policy. You may be better off keeping the old policy and purchasing a new one on top of it, if you are trying to add inflation coverage. Your insurance agent can advise you on the best thing to do. Whatever you do, never cancel an existing policy until a new one is in effect.

Your Customized Benefit Selection Process

To simplify the benefit selection process, you just need to remember that there are six major choices that impact a premium. Here is each choice and a recommendation.

1) Daily or Monthly Benefit—Look at the average cost in your area and buy a daily or monthly benefit as high as you can afford—even $20-$30 more than the average cost in your area if you can afford it. Inflation is strong, and you'll probably need the extra benefit at claim time. (The national average cost for semi-private room and board is $157 per day including miscellaneous charges—"high cost areas" like Alaska and parts of New England and California average $300 per day, including miscellaneous charges.)[13] A private room usually costs $10-$20 more per day than a semi-private.

If you are planning on self-insuring some of the cost, don't forget to account for the average of 20% or so for additional charges like drugs and miscellaneous supplies that are billed in addition to the room and board rate. Prescription drugs represent the biggest chunk of that, so if you have other coverage for prescription drugs you won't need to budget as much as 20% extra.

Some insurance agents may be able to provide you with a local cost survey, or you can call some providers listed in the Yellow Pages: assisted living facilities, home health agencies, adult day care centers and nursing homes. Your local Agency on Aging also may have this information. You can get that number by calling your state's Agency on Aging office. (See **Appendix B,** *Who to Call for Help.*)

Cost surveys normally will reflect just the room and board rate for nursing home care, not the additional charges for drugs and supplies. Most reimbursement policies will pay no more than the room and board charge and you are on your own for these miscellaneous charges. An indemnity policy that pays the selected daily or monthly benefit regardless of charge makes it possible to build in extra benefit to cover the extra charges. Most policies are reimbursement, because the theory is that people will use insurance more wisely if there is some cost sharing and a wiser use of benefits will help hold rates down in the future.

2) Waiting Period (Elimination Period)—Most people will choose a waiting period (deductible) of 100 days or less. If you have over $1 million in assets (not counting your house and car), you can look at waiting periods of greater than 100 days. (Some states allow insurance companies to offer waiting periods as long as 180, 365 or even 730 days.) If you have assets less than $100,000, definitely choose a shorter waiting period like 20 or 30 days. If you have assets greater than $100,000 most companies offer waiting periods of 60 days, 90 days or 100 days. (The premium difference between 20 and 100 days with most companies is about 20%, so you have to contrast that with self-insuring the cost for an additional 80 days—not just at today's costs but at future costs.) Look at policies that require only one waiting period in a lifetime.

Assets * *Does not include house and car	Suggested Waiting Period (in days)		
	20–30	60–90	100+
Under $100,000	X		
$100,000– $500,000	X	X	
Over $500,000			X

A few policies do not require formal charges during the waiting period. If you are considering that type of policy, the question becomes "How long can I *wait* before benefits begin vs. how long can I *pay*"—in other words, how long could you manage with help from informal caregivers, like family and friends before benefits start?

3) Benefit Period/Benefit Maximum—Choose at least two years and longer if you can afford it, but don't ever sacrifice inflation coverage for a longer benefit period. If you live in a "Partnership" state (Connecticut, New York, Indiana, California, Illinois, or Washington) see **The Partnership for Long-Term Care** on p. 119 for guidance.

4) Inflation Protection—The method that makes your benefit grow 5% compounded every year for the rest of your life is *nonnegotiable* if you are age 70 or under. If you are in your early 70's, you can choose the method that makes your benefit grow 5% of the original amount (5% simple) for the rest of your life, if your state allows that option. If your state doesn't allow it, purchase the 5% compound. If you are in the upper 70's or older, you can purchase an extra benefit—perhaps an extra $30-$50 per day—to build in immediate inflation protection.

5) Home Health and Community Coverage—If you have someone to live with who can be a primary caregiver, you can select this coverage if it is optional on the policy you are considering. Some policies include it and it's not an option. If you do not have a primary caregiver and home health care benefits are required, the policy may allow you to lower your premium by choosing a reduced percentage such as 50%. If you are younger (30's–50's) and you don't know if you will have a primary caregiver, buy it if you can afford it so you will have maximum choice when you need care.

Note: If you have no one to live with, you may be better off buying a "Facility Only" policy with "cadillac" benefit levels, such as private room coverage, 5% compound inflation, lifetime benefit period, and the like. Not everyone is a candidate for home health benefits. One of my clients is a retired schoolteacher with no family. If she needs extensive help, she absolutely does not want to stay home. We used her premium dollars to purchase the best assisted living/nursing home policy she could afford. Bill Comfort, Jr., an agent in St. Louis, had a similar story:

> *After a lengthy discussion of all the wonderful long-term care insurance policy features that would allow for her to stay in her own home, a new client of mine looked at me and said, "If I ever need this kind of help, I don't want to stay in my own home."*

> *I couldn't believe it. Doesn't everyone want to stay in their own home as long as possible? No. My client is a single woman with no family in town. She knew that if she needed on-going long-term care that it would be time to move—part of life. We found a policy with the best assisted living and nursing facility benefits she could get.*

6) Non-Forfeiture—This benefit is something you can do without. It increases your premium significantly with very little value in return. The extra 30% or so you would spend for this option is better spent on purchasing the 5% inflation rider or if you are 75 or older, at least a higher daily benefit to combat inflation or a longer benefit period if you've already taken care of inflation.

The Bare-Bones/Best Value Policy
for the Premium Conscious

Summary: If premium is your main consideration, the most "bare-bones" policy with the best premium value for the dollar is a policy that pays:

▲   assisted living and nursing home only, sometimes called a "Facility Only" policy
▲   a 20-or 30-day waiting period
▲   a two or three-year benefit period
▲   the appropriate inflation choice for your age (see "Inflation Protection" p. 90).

You can delete the home care as long as assisted living is covered. **Do not delete the inflation coverage.** If your benefit is too small at claim time and you can't make up the difference, you could wind up on Medicaid immediately (or whatever type of public assistance/welfare benefit is available at the time).

Some Parting Advice

Many companies are competing for your premium dollar, so don't fall prey to marketing strategies that may cause unnecessary rate increases in the future. Companies that offer very low premiums compared to most of the other companies, sell policies to people with significant health problems, and make it very easy to obtain benefits (see *Claims* p. 75) are at a higher than average risk for rate increases—particularly if the company is small. (There are companies selling long-term care insurance with $100 million in assets and there are companies with $100 billion and more in assets.)

You can also call your insurance department to ask about earlier rate increase activity as well as any complaints that have been filed against the insurance company. (See **Appendix B** for the contact information for your state's insurance department.)

Chapter 3

Long-Term Care:
The New Employee Benefit

∖∖∖∖∖∖∖∖∖∖∖∖∖∖∖∖∖∖∖∖∖∖∖∖∖∖∖∖∖∖∖∖∖∖

With the emergence of four-generation families, the future is going to be filled with double-decker sandwiched generations. As a result, the average 21st-century American will actually spend more years caring for parents than children.[1]

—*Dr. Ken Dychtwald,* AgePower

Over 3,000 employers in the United States offered long-term care insurance to their employees in 1999, and almost one-third in the previous year made a contribution to the premium.[2] This number is expected to explode in the next century, when elder care is projected to replace child care as the #1 dependent care issue in the United States by 2005, when 1 out of 3 workers will be more concerned with caring for a parent than a child.[3] If that sounds like *Future Shock* and something that can't possibly come true in our lifetime, think again. A recent AARP study said just over 23% of all U.S. households have provided care to a relative or friend over 50 years old in the fall of 1996, and three-fourths of these are currently providing care. The report further said the number of households in the United States providing elder care has tripled since 1988—in other words, in less than a decade![4]

The fuse to encourage employers to offer long-term care insurance was lit by 1996 health care reform. Benefits from policies issued 1/1/97 and later are tax-free to employees whether the employee or the employer pays the premium. Premium contributions are now a business expense to employers and are not classified as taxable income to employees. With employer-sponsored plans having tripled in the last five years,[5] the new laws should propel the number of employers on the fence about long-term care insurance to make it available to huge numbers of Americans in the very near future.

If legislation is the fuse, employee demand is the bomb, and it is exploding.

▲ Two-thirds of the employees who participated in a 1999 National Council on Aging/John Hancock Survey reported they would like long-term care insurance to be offered at their workplaces.[6]

▲ Long-term care insurance was the single benefit most desired by employees in the William M. Mercer, Inc. 1998 Survey on Employee Benefit Preferences.[7]

▲ Respondents to a 1998 UNUM survey said they were more likely to buy long-term care insurance through their employers than if they had to buy it on their own.[8]

Employers are responding to the outcry. Although only 15 percent of employers currently offer long-term care coverage in a recent survey, the great news is that 48% of the group not offering group LTC insurance may offer it in the future.[9]

What is driving this intense and urgent demand from employees? Quite simply, it's the caregiving needs in their personal lives that threaten to eclipse their professional lives.

Consider that 5.75 million Americans are in the "sandwich generation" of caring for both children and parents,[10] and out of that is hatching caregiving demands unlike our society has ever known. Forty-two percent of employees surveyed in 1998 expect to assume elder-care duties over the next five years[11] and a 1998 national public opinion poll showed that more than half of Americans say it is likely they will be responsible for the care of an elderly parent or relative in the next ten years.[12] A National Council on Aging/Pew Trust study predicts that the roughly 3.3 million baby boomers now providing long-distance care will more than double over the next 15 years.[13]

And finally, two-thirds of employees who responded to the 1999 National Council on Aging/John Hancock Survey agree that LTC is the greatest threat to their standard of living in retirement.[14]

As baby boomers are watching the phenomenal emotional and financial price exacted on parents and grandparents who haven't planned ahead, the result is a generation that is demanding a better way. Existing health insurance and Medicare don't pay for long-term care, and the dependent care benefit that allows employees to set aside $5,000 tax-free annually for elder or child care is just a drop in a bottomless bucket with long-term care averaging $50,000 a year on up. So employees in all size companies are searching for answers through long-term care insurance.

Surprisingly, the largest growth is in small firms. Two-thirds of the companies offering long-term care plans in 1998 had less than 500 employees, and half had 100 or less.[15] This is probably happening for two reasons:

    small companies feel the productivity loss caused by caregiving needs more dramatically than large employers; and

    small business owners can react to a problem and make quicker decisions than large companies.

This trend will be stimulated as more people who are self-employed or who work for a company with 50 or less employees understand that long-term care insurance can be paid for with pre-tax dollars through the new Medical Savings Accounts (see p. 24 in **Long-Term Care and Your Financial Security**).

There are several kinds of long-term care insurance plans are available today.

A growing number of insurance companies are offering their individual long-term care insurance product to small employers, all the way down to a minimum of three applications in a group. While employees have to be in reasonably good health to be eligible, the company usually provides a payroll deduction discount of 10%–15%. This is especially great if the coverage also is offered to parents and in-laws. An employee who terminates employment can keep the policy and usually the group discount as well.

Group long-term care insurance offered through larger employers typically allows the employee to get coverage without checking the employee's health. (A few plans treat the spouse the same way.) This "guaranteed issue" coverage for the employee normally is available only to large employers, but at least one insurance company offers it to employers as small as 200 employees. At least six other companies offer a similar version for companies with 100 employees down to as small as 25 employees (and one company as small as 10) with only two or three health questions, such as "Do you need help with activities of daily living (bathing, dressing, eating, toileting, continence, transferring from bed to chair)," "Do you have AIDS?" and "Have you been declined for long-term care insurance?" Assuming the employee is actively at work and the answer to the questions is "No," the employee is approved for a policy. A couple of these small group plans will even provide a small policy to employees who are declined for health reasons.[16]

Plans for larger employers usually offer coverage to employees, spouses, parents, in-laws, and some plans even offer coverage to grandparents. The good news is that for family members, the medical underwriting may be less restrictive than for individual long-term care policies. In most companies the employee's portion of the premium is automatically deducted from his or her paycheck via payroll deduction. Parents and in-laws may be billed directly. If the employee terminates employment or retires, the policy is portable and the employee may keep the coverage, usually at the same premium. Coverage is generally available from age 18 to age 79, and some have no maximum age limit.

Employees are buying long-term care insurance for two reasons: to help with the escalating need for elder care, and for their own long-term care needs. Let's address the need for elder care first.

Productivity Insurance

The National Alliance for Caregiving/AARP study referenced earlier reports that three-fourths of households in America that have had a caregiver in the last twelve months are still providing care. That's about 11,000,000 caregivers and two-thirds of these caregivers are employed full or part-time.[17] This means that almost 10% of the workforce today provide care for someone over 50, and as noted on p. 97, 42% expect to have caregiving responsibilities in the next five years. These numbers do not even count the number of caregivers who are providing care for the 40% of Americans needing long-term care who are working-age adults, ages 18-64.[18] How will productivity be affected by these staggering long-term care needs?

The National Alliance for Caregiving/AARP study portrayed the following list of sacrifices made by employed caregivers who provided help with two or more Activities of Daily Living for an average of 56 hours a week.[19]

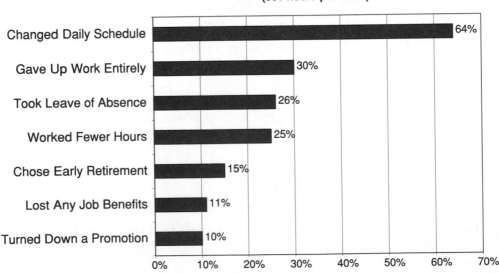

Work-Related Adjustments for Most Intense Caregivers
(56+ hours per week)

Of *all* caregivers, 54% had to make changes at work to accommodate caregiving, but 64% of the most intense caregivers had to make changes to their daily work schedule, 30% had to give up work entirely, 15% took early retirement and 26% had to take a leave of absence. The Conference Board, a well-known employee benefits "think tank," estimates replacement costs to be 75% of the annual salary of the employee who quits.[20]

Born in 1919 and married at 15 to Everett Corker, Margie Evelyn Bowles Corker devoted her life to motherhood. She raised her children, Justine and Bill, with strength of character, teaching them to respect others and to aspire to high values and the reflective behavior. When Terri and Perry put in their surprise appearance 20 years after Justine, she hadn't changed—they got the same "schoolin'"as their older brother and sister. Statistically, they beat the odds—not one black sheep out of a flock of four. Margie wondered when Terri, the younger of the twins, turned toward music, and she really worried when Terri left home to tour with a popular singer.

Her fears were groundless. Terri's straight-arrow upbringing didn't fit with life on the road where booze and drugs were the roadmap. When lung cancer took Everett in a few short months in 1983, West Virginia didn't seem as confining, but Terri knew the music couldn't happen there. A few years after his death, she made the move to Nashville, with Margie in tow, who was already using a crutch due to the instability caused by degenerating arthritis. Her mother refused to drive in the big city, and the role reversal began.

Renting an apartment with her mother, Terri couldn't afford the footloose, hand-to-mouth existence of many Nashville musicians, nor did she want to live that way. She advanced in her day job to Operations Manager with an industrial supply firm and worked the songwriter venues nights and weekends. After several years of dues-paying, some of her original songs were recorded and things looked promising. Then Margie's health began to fail rapidly. Terri gave up a weekly songwriter night she had hosted for two years and began to pass paying music "gigs" to other musicians. Her first CD coincided with a blur of breast cancer, surgeries due to severe arthritis, pneumonia, congestive heart failure and an endless stream of multiple medications. The CD bypassed the back seat and went into the trunk of her life. Personal relationships came and went as Terri's first priority was to Margie. She wrote three new songs instead of 10 the following year. Terri saved furiously, knowing what was ahead, even though she had to pay a sitter three hours a day to help Margie with her meals. She never returned to work after a four-month leave of absence from her job in 1998 while Margie underwent extensive radiation treatments.

After Margie's death in January 2000, the eight year circus finally ended. Five months after the funeral, Terri is still looking for the identity she feels she has lost through it all. She doesn't regret the time with her mother in any way—she's just trying to assess where she is at age 42 with her career, her personal life, and what's left after the many years of caregiving that brought her to this point. Her motto "The only routine is there is none" no longer applies. Have the years of caregiving stolen her dream for a music career?

Even long-distance caregivers who don't do the most intense caregiving and live more than an hour away from their older family members devote an average of 35 hours a month, equal to nearly one work week, to providing or arranging housekeeping, meals and other services for these aging family members, says a National Council on Aging study. Fifteen percent of these "long-distance caregivers" report taking unpaid leave from work, and have been helping out an average 5.1 years.[21]

The really astounding bird's-eye view is that among all caregivers, not just intense or long-distance, 21% have provided care for five to nine years, and 10% for 10 years or more.[22]

Caregivers' Responsibilities

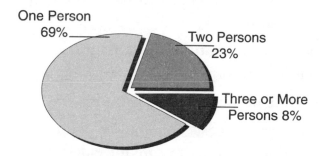

Seven in 10 caregivers provide care to just one person, but 23% take care of two people, and eight percent care for three or more people![23]

Caregiving Periods

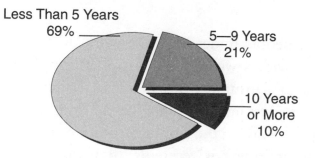

Caregiving responsibilities have a number of hidden impacts on job performance and overall company expenses, including:[24]

△   workday interruptions to handle emergencies and phone calls

△   absenteeism

△   increased employee stress often resulting in health-related problems

△   increased necessity for time off and leaves from work

△   decreased willingness to relocate or travel for work

△   decisions to cut back to part-time or leave the work force altogether

△   decrease in motivation and morale due to pressures outside the workplace

△   decline in productivity

△   replacement costs ("employees who cut back or leave positions in order to care for elders average between 5 and 17 percent depending on the company")

The annual price tag for employers is somewhere around $30 billion,[25] but this list just adds up to one big word for the employee: Stress.

Since most people under 65 must work, long-term care insurance can provide a wonderful solution to employees with elder care needs. LTC insurance provides financial assistance, which in turn reduces stress levels by allowing the employee to keep his or her job, and by giving the employee peace of mind knowing that the parent or in-law is receiving high quality care while the employee is at work.

What if you can't afford to pay your parent's premium by yourself? JoAnn Canning, a New York City-based long-term care specialist, reports in the January 4, 1993 issue of *National Underwriter* that "when children enter into a 'multiple support' agreement (under which they agree to provide funds for the parent so that the parent can be claimed as a dependent for income tax purposes) they can also join in purchasing an LTC policy for the parent."

This way, the LTC policy can relieve both children's and parents' anxiety by making sure that many choices for care exist when needed, i.e., alternatives to nursing home care, which is usually the only option when the patient is on Medicaid. The LTC policy also acts to safeguard the children's inheritance instead of spending the parents' savings on long-term care expenses. Many attorneys recommend LTC policies for this reason.

Thanks to the recent health care reform legislation, a portion of the premium based on the parent's age is counted as a medical expense and becomes a potential tax deduction for the child paying the premium, as long as the parent is a dependent. (This just means the child or children must provide greater than 50% of the parent's support.) In the case of multiple support agreements as explained above, one child each year can take the tax deduction as long as that child contributed at least 10% of the parent's support for that tax year.

The wave of the future is companies like Lancaster Labs in Lancaster, Pennsylvania, which offers on-site adult day care at a reasonable cost to employees of $33 per day, in addition to child care. Long-term care insurance will pay for adult day care. How many insurance policies will pay for child care?

Robert Ridgley, chairman of Northwest Natural Gas, a Portland, Oregon, utility, is another example of an employer who recognizes how serious long-term care is for his employees. His company surveyed 1,350 workers about child-care needs, only to find that "We had as many or more people spending a significant amount of time and emotional capital on elder care."[26]

Lifestyle Insurance

Numbers like this affect all segments of society, but the fastest growing segment of corporate America—small business—has a huge stake in this problem. Many Americans look forward to getting their children at least in high school or even through college, and then experiencing "The American Dream"—starting the business they've always dreamed of. Starting a business usually means long hours—60+ hours a week is not unusual for the entrepreneur. Suddenly, a spouse, parent, or in-law has an accident or a stroke, and caregiving becomes the #1 priority. The dream never happens.

Bev Fulkerson is 42. On the surface, her life seems to be going well. She just got a promotion to state director of a new suicide prevention grant for a crisis intervention center in Nashville, Tennessee. Without talking with her, you wouldn't know how deeply she appreciates being back in the workforce with a meaningful job. Her appreciation is tinged with sadness, however, because it means she isn't running her own private practice as an addictions/mental health counselor for adolescents, a business she tried to start six months ago.

Two years ago, her energetic 72-year-old mother, known for her pep, spunk and tremendous sense of humor, entered a

Louisville, Kentucky, hospital for a routine heart bypass. Her father's similar surgery a year earlier had kept him in the hospital a mere five days. The day of the surgery, Bev accepted a new job as director of a counseling center just outside of Nashville that catered to adolescents. After 16 years in the field, she was ecstatic.

Her mother came home 12 ½ months later.

Allergic to the medications used during surgery, her recovery time stretched past two months. Just as she was being transferred to the rehabilitation wing, she couldn't shake the feeling that something was wrong, that the wound wasn't healing properly. She had a staph infection, a phrase that strikes terror to anyone in the medical profession, especially the people who handle the billing and the legal functions. Did the hospital cause it? Will the exorbitant bill be paid in full? (Mrs. Fulkerson's bill went over $2 million.)

It was five more months before the actual rehabilitation treatment could begin and another three before she was transferred to an independent skilled nursing facility in Louisville. She was there 3½ months before coming home, unable to walk or even turn herself in bed. She began eight months of home health care which ended in mid-April, 2000. Today her youthful looks have dissipated, she has lost 70 pounds, and her sense of humor is a dim light in the distance. In the midst of the hospital stay, Bev was successful at getting an anti-depressant prescribed for her mother only after four months of insisting and a meeting with the hospital administrator, a feat which deeply underscores the need for family advocacy even when someone is in a medical facility.

Bev was lucky. Her younger brother in Louisville took a three-month family leave when the problems began and has been extremely supportive during the entire episode. Bev was able to keep her job by commuting to Louisville, two hours away, every weekend and usually at least once during the week for two years.

Last December, when it looked like Mrs. Fulkerson might actually come out of it, Bev decided to go for her big dream, which was to start her own private practice as an adolescent counselor. By January, she was ready to go. Then her father discovered a lump in his groin, and was diagnosed with lymphoma. Her mother couldn't be left alone during the weeks of extensive testing, so for Bev, the nightmare began all over again.

The good news is that the lymphoma appears to be dormant so no ongoing treatment is necessary and Bev is free to return to the workforce. The bad news is that financially she no longer has the resources to start her own practice. In her words, "The dream of having a private practice went out the back window. Anything I wanted to do or needed to do for myself is put on the back burner."

The following caregiver wasn't so fortunate.

Linda, a 48-year-old supervisor at a bank and a divorced mother of two children in college, had planned a very different life for herself. Five years ago she was anticipating her youngest child's departure for college and looking forward to a new personal chapter in her life—a chapter that included more time for herself, a chance to study art history and perhaps even a second career. Instead, her mother, previously an independent and active widow in her early 70's, was diagnosed with Alzheimer's disease. Since then, Linda's dreams have ceased to exist. Her mother has lived with her three years, with Linda footing the bill for adult day care so she can continue working. The strain on her budget is unbelievable, especially when combined with the cost of drugs and a few other medical services not covered by Medicare.

Linda also had never imagined how difficult things would be as a result of no personal time. She misses her shopping trips, movies with her friends and is frustrated by her inability to attend parent functions at her children's colleges. But the hardest part is the isolation she feels. She doesn't want people at work to think she's down all the time.

The caregiving responsibilities Linda has undertaken will continue to increase, especially now that her mom has started wandering at all hours.

The above caregiving story is an excerpt from the National Family Caregivers Association (NFCA)/Fortis Report, members of which are primarily involved in intense caregiving situations. Nearly half were employed and three-fourths of them worked more than 30 hours per week. The average length of time these working caregivers have been providing care is 7.9 years and 28% have been at it longer than 10 years. Half of the remaining caregivers expect to be providing care more than ten years!

The most reported emotion is a sense of isolation, even among the employed, because, like Linda, they probably feel as though they have to be "up" while on the job.

Three out of five of these caregivers reported they were depressed as a result of their caregiving activities, a number that is six times the national average for clinical depression. Younger caregivers in their 30's and 40's especially reported depression and particularly those who provided care more than 40 hours a week, which almost half do.

The caregivers in the NCFA report were a mixture, with half of them caring for a spouse, a fourth for a parent, 20% for a child and remaining caregivers took care of a sibling or friend. Of all of them, children caring for parents have the highest depression and lowest feelings of inner strength. The three greatest difficulties the adult children named were role reversal, isolation, and loss of leisure time.[27]

Take a look at this chart from *USA Today* that illustrates the sacrifices made by adults age 35–54 who have provided long-term care for family or friends.[28]

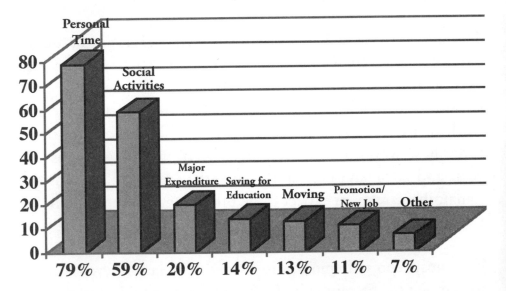

The 1999 National Council on Aging/John Hancock survey reported that more than one-quarter of respondents providing financial assistance for a friend or relative has used their retirement savings and 12% used money set aside for a child's education. Nineteen percent gave up a job to provide care, while another 19% took a second job.[29]

It's easy to see from these numbers that caregivers often suffer significant drops in income as a result of a caregiving situation. In a follow-up study of 55 of the most intense caregivers from the study referenced above, Metropolitan Life Insurance Company was able to quantify an average total lost wealth amount of $659,139 due to the intense caregiving situation ($566,443 lost wages, which caused an average of $25,494 in lost Social Security benefits since they couldn't work as much and earn as much, and for those eligible, losses in pension benefits averaging $67,202). The average caregiving time of these 55 intense caregivers is eight years, but one-third have provided care for ten or more years.[30]

What sacrifices were made in both time and money in these families? How did each individual family member suffer? How welcome would a home health aide providing at least 40 hours of care per week have been?

The typical caregiver in the National Alliance for Caregiving/ AARP study is a married woman in her mid-forties who works full-time. In another major survey, employed caregivers providing care for severely disabled individuals (3 or more ADLs)[31] reported an average of 36.9 hours worked each week and 32–39 hours of caregiving each week on top of the work week. Respondents to the National Council on Aging/John Hancock survey provide hands-on care an average of 41 hours a week, but 22% provide 50 hours or more.[32]

How do you function in an executive position or grow your own business with those kind of hours? Now let's throw in another dimension. The really hard part comes when caring for children and parents or grandparents happens simultaneously. (Forty-one percent of caregivers in the AARP study had one or more children under age 18 living at home.)[33]

Because the predominant number of caregivers are women, caregiving may turn out to be the biggest threat to the women's movement in the next century. Even today, the average 21st Century American is projected to spend more years taking care of aging family members than raising children.[34]

Here is an example of what the incredible pressure from both ends looks like:

> *Jenny is an example of multigenerational caregiving. Jenny and her husband provide support for her 88-year-old mother and her husband's 89-year-old mother, and their 28-year-old daughter just moved back home with her three children ages 6 and under. Jenny's name was on a prayer request list.*[35]

Families can't do it alone. They have to have help, and long-term care insurance may be the main key to the help they need, in addition to lots of prayers! The AARP study says "prayer is the most common way of coping with the stresses and strains of caregiving— almost three in four caregivers (74%) use this method."[36] Future long-term care insurance policies may earn the name "lifestyle insurance," because the policy may be the only thing that allows an adult child to continue a career or even keep a marriage from falling apart from the strain of a caregiving need of a very long duration.

Well-known columnist Terry Savage from the *Chicago Sun-Times* wrote about buying long-term care insurance on her parents in the June/July 2000 issue of *Mirabella* magazine:

> *When I bought a policy for each of my parents as a holiday gift a few years ago, the reaction was predictable. My father smiled and thanked me . . . and then went out for a jog. My mother's reaction was a little more emotional: "After your grandmother, you promised you'd never . . ." The words trailed off as we both remembered. Then I smiled at her and reminded her that this policy would pay for someone to come into her home and give needed care. We'd never have to face the issue of a nursing home (I hope and pray). And if we do, I know I've ensured her the best of care. That's why I also bought a policy for myself.*

Long-term care happens not to an individual. It happens to the entire family, and this popular columnist sees this clearly.

Long-Term Care Insurance Is Not "Senior Citizen Insurance"

Long-Term Care and Your Financial Security explained there is a 1 out of 2 chance of needing either home health care or nursing home care at some point in your life.[37] The two-edged sword of long-term care is that it can be needed at any age. As noted on p. 98, 40% of Americans needing long-term care today are working age adults ages 18-64![38] Only about 10% of nursing home patients are under 65,[39] so most of these younger people needing long-term care are being cared for in the community, at a very large sacrifice for family members. Consider these actual cases:

▲   a 29-year-old had a massive stroke a month before her wedding day. Her fiance continues to care for her 11 years later—her mind is fine, but she communicates with her eyes and is confined to a wheelchair. They live with her parents.[40]

▲   a 25-year-old Cookeville, Tennessee, man who slammed into the side of a dump truck that pulled out in front of his motorcycle was discharged from a nursing home seven months later after an extended coma, then spent the next three years relearning every skill he was born with—his wife's life stopped with his as she stayed by his side throughout.[41]

▲   a 49-year-old Nashville woman still raising her 11-year-old son, is bed-ridden in her 11th year of Lou Gehrig's disease. Her muscles and body virtually petri-fied, she taps out Morse Code through sensors attached by Velcro to her fingertips, which signal a laptop com-puter to write and speak her thoughts through a syn-thesized voice.[42]

And consider the nursing home stories of younger people:

▲   a 58-year-old Illinois man who has been in a nursing home since an aneurysm at age 49.[43]

▲   an Illinois woman lying comatose in a nursing home after suffering a stroke during childbirth in her late 30's.[43]

▲   a 26-year-old in a coma after an automobile accident in which he was forced off the road by the driver of the car he was passing who was angry because he forgot to dim his headlights.[43]

A quick reminder: Conventional group health insurance does not cover long-term care because it covers mainly skilled care in a nursing home or at home, and almost all long-term care is not skilled. People who just need help with bathing, getting in and out of bed, taking medicine, toileting, eating, etc. do not receive payment for this type of help from conventional health insurance. A perfect example of someone who needs this type of help and who is not helped by traditional health insurance is someone who is paralyzed from an accident or stroke. Once the patient settles into a chronic, maintenance state and just needs help with basic activities of daily living, payment for caregiving stops under regular health insurance.

Many younger people think disability income insurance takes care of them. Disability income coverage just provides money with which to pay bills (mortgage, utilities, food, etc.) and does not provide an extra $3,000-$6,000 a month to pay for long-term care expenses.

A Health Insurance Association of America survey reports that the average age of employees who have purchased long-term care insurance is 43.[44] Younger people are more likely to see long-term care insurance as just another part of their plan for retirement. The money accumulated in pension plans, 401K, investments, annuities, real estate, etc., is in jeopardy if long-term care is needed. The 40-year-old today is facing long-term care expenses of almost $550,000 per year in forty years if present trends continue with an annual growth rate of 5.8%, and that's a conservative figure.[45]

Tips for Benefit Choices in Group Plans

Group long-term care plans are similar to individual policies, but there are a few specific areas you should check before deciding on a plan:

Inflation Coverage—You may be offered a plan with or without inflation coverage. **BUY INFLATION COVERAGE.** There are different types of inflation coverage. For example, you may be offered a plan with low premiums now and a chance to buy additional coverage in the future. Usually, if you have a claim, these offers are withdrawn. If you are offered the opportunity to buy a plan that guarantees your daily or monthly benefit will grow automatically each year as long as you hold the policy, take it. The premium will be more than the other kind in the beginning, but you will pay much less over the long haul and your benefit has a much better chance of keeping up with the rising cost of long-term care. Also, if you have a claim, your benefit will continue to grow and in most plans, your premium will stop. Select the automatic increase option that grows compounded (not simple) each year and only the benefit should increase annually, not the premium.

Home Health Care—Many group plans offer benefits that cover long-term care outside of the nursing home, such as home health care, adult day care, foster home care, etc. as an option. You are well advised to take it because even today, nursing home care only makes up about 15% of the long-term care picture.[46] It is expected that since nursing home beds are less than 90% occupied today, that research will provide more and more ways to provide future long-term care in the community.[47] Most people would rather be cared for at home as long as possible, anyway. If you have a choice between a home care benefit that pays less than the nursing home benefit (i.e., 50%) and one that pays equal to the nursing home benefit, choose the one that is equal (the best choice), or at least 75%-80%, since home care costs can equal and even exceed nursing home costs.

Non-forfeiture/Return of Premium Benefits—Many group plans offer an option that allows you (or your beneficiary) to get your premiums back or keep some of the benefit if you cancel your policy or die without using it. Extra premium is charged for this privilege, so analyze carefully if the extra premium is a wise expenditure. The odds are great that you will use the coverage, never get any money back, and you will have paid the extra premium for nothing. You might be better off putting the extra premium in your 401K or other retirement fund or a mutual fund, etc., or use it to buy a higher level of benefit: an increased dollar amount of coverage, or better inflation or home care benefits.

Here is a summary of why employees are buying long-term care insurance:

1) To take care of their own long-term care needs, as the need can occur at any age.

2) To help with elder care needs so they can continue working while taking care of aging family members.

3) To take advantage of lower premiums for themselves at younger ages and underwriting concessions for the employee, in particular since the employee usually gets covered with no health questions, and for any available underwriting breaks for family members who may find

it more difficult to qualify medically for individual LTC policies.

4) To help the private sector fund the long-term care crisis, because the more people who wind up in nursing homes on Medicaid (welfare), the higher our taxes will be to help the government pay the bill. (Sweden has a national long-term care program and a tax rate of about 58%!)[48]

You may be able to enroll in a group or association long-term care plan by mail, but you and your spouse should attend any meetings held by your employer or association as well so you will get a first-hand explanation of long-term care issues and the products being offered. Your parents and in-laws are usually welcome at these educational meetings.

Whether you review group or individual long-term care policies— **DON'T WAIT** to purchase a policy. American families desperately need to prepare today for a long-term care need that could strike at any time.

Chapter 4

The Partnership for Long-Term Care

~~~~~~

The Partnership for Long-Term Care is a public/private alliance between state governments and insurance companies that was originally funded with $14 million in grants from the nation's largest health care philanthropy, the Robert Wood Johnson Foundation. The program is operational in Connecticut, New York, Indiana, California and approved in Iowa. Variations of the Partnership are operational in Illinois, Massachusetts and Washington.

The idea of the partnership is to provide a way for the Medicaid program to work together with private long-term care insurance to help those people who are caught in the middle: they can't afford to pay the cost of the care or even the cost of a long-term care insurance policy with unlimited benefits, yet their assets are too high to qualify for Medicaid to pay their long-term care expenses. Many middle-income workers and retirees also find themselves in this position.

Participating insurance companies in the Partnership recognize the needs of these middle-income Americans by providing LTC insurance policies that have built-in consumer protection benefit standards, and participating states cooperate by allowing these policyholders to get Medicaid without spending down their assets almost to poverty level if the insurance benefits run out. Without the Partnership, people have three choices to pay for long-term care:

1) Pay for care out of assets and income, which can lead to financial ruin if long-term care costs wipe out savings.

2) Transfer assets to qualify for Medicaid either to children or other family members or to a trust—either way means losing control of the money and losing financial independence.

3) Buy a standard long-term care insurance policy which works—unless the policy runs out of benefits or the benefit isn't enough to cover the cost of care. This can happen because you bought what you could afford, and it turns out not to be enough when you need it. (For example, you couldn't afford the premium for inflation coverage or you could only afford a one- or two-year benefit period.)

A fourth option is available with the Partnership for Long-Term Care. Now consumers can purchase a state-approved LTC policy that provides asset protection after the benefits run out. Here's how it works in all of the above-mentioned states except New York.

▲   You purchase a special Partnership policy from an insurance agent. For every dollar in benefits paid by the policy, you can shelter a dollar in assets. For example, let's say you buy a two-year benefit period because that's what you can afford. If this policy pays, say,

$60,000 in benefits, and if the Medicaid asset eligibility in your state requires you to spend down to $2,000, in this example you would be able to qualify for Medicaid when your assets reach $62,000, not $2,000. In other words, you get to keep, or "shelter" $60,000 of your assets and still get Medicaid to start paying your long-term care expenses after your policy runs out.

▲   In New York, Partnership policies must cover three years of nursing home benefits or six years of home care (or a combination of both), and once the benefits are exhausted, the policyholder can qualify for Medicaid regardless of the amount of assets.

While New York offers unlimited asset protection, this desirable feature only happens after you have used up the benefits of the policy. A danger is that if you purchase a daily benefit that is inadequate for your needs, you could use up your assets paying the difference between your policy's benefit and the cost of care before your benefits are used up.

For example, in 2001 New York requires new Partnership policy purchasers to purchase a minimum of $148 for the daily benefit. The New York City metropolitan area averages $295[1], not counting the miscellaneous charges for drugs and medical supplies. If you only buy the minimum, you could easily wind up paying $150 per day or more out of your pocket, which amounts to over $160,000 over the three-year benefit period for nursing home care. The New York State Partnership for Long-Term Care reported the following averages for room and board for New York in 1999:

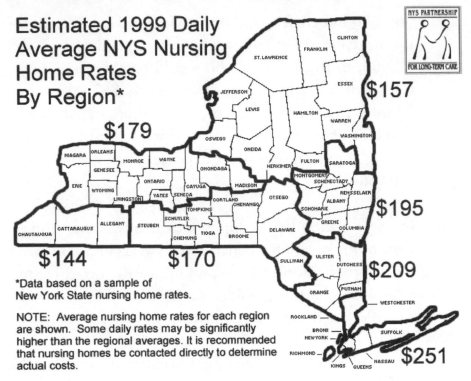

Estimated 1999 Daily Average NYS Nursing Home Rates By Region*

$157

$179

$195

$144 $170 $209

$251

*Data based on a sample of New York State nursing home rates.

NOTE: Average nursing home rates for each region are shown. Some daily rates may be significantly higher than the regional averages. It is recommended that nursing homes be contacted directly to determine actual costs.

▲ Illinois and Indiana provide a combination of these two models. The combo plan provides the dollar-for-dollar asset protection just as it does now for all of the states except New York, but if the policyholder purchases a benefit maximum that will pay about four years of benefits, the policy will provide total asset protection like the New York model. Since $162,068 represents about four years of benefits at current costs, purchasing a policy that would pay out that much in benefits would qualify you for the total asset protection feature in Indiana. (The $162,068 is the 2001 amount and will increase each year to account for inflation.) An insurance agent who is approved to sell Partnership policies can help you identify the best combination of benefits for your needs. The Indiana Partnership maintains a list of agents who have had special Partnership training. Call the Indiana Partnership telephone number listed at the end of this chapter for a directory of approved agents.

In all states, your income goes to pay for the cost of care once you qualify for Medicaid. So the Partnership program protects assets, not income. But income is important for three reasons:

1) If your income is greater than your long-term care costs, you won't qualify for Medicaid and wouldn't benefit from a Partnership policy. People in this situation can consider a standard long-term care insurance policy— perhaps with an unlimited benefit maximum.

2) Income can guide you to a benefit selection. For example, if nursing home care costs $120 per day in your area, and you can afford to pay $20 a day from your income, you might purchase a policy for $100 a day for a lower premium than a $120/day policy. (In higher cost areas like New York, Connecticut or California, you would probably be purchasing policies in the $250+/day range.) Just be careful—if your care costs more than the insurance policy pays in benefits, you will be responsible for paying the additional costs, and don't forget that drugs and medical supplies are usually billed on top of the room and board charge. Consider carefully how much you can afford to pay out of your income and insure yourself adequately. The Partnership policies include an inflation benefit for appropriate ages so that inflation doesn't erode your benefit.

3) Since you are responsible for paying your premiums, your discretionary income must be sufficient to pay your long-term care premiums and keep your policy in force, although there is a premium waiver if you have a claim. Individuals with income less than $20,000 or couples with incomes less than $40,000 may not have enough discretionary income to purchase long-term care insurance as premium payments may significantly impact their standard of living. If you fall into these income categories, and if you have assets less than $50,000, not counting your house and car, you probably will qualify for Medicaid in a short period of time, and LTC insurance of any type—standard or Partnership—may not be an appropriate purchase for you.

For many people, the Partnership LTC policies offer a wonderful alternative to transferring assets and relying on the government (Medicaid) to pay for their long-term care expenses. In addition to the legal pitfalls (see **The Medicaid Benefit for Long-Term Care**, p. 129), there are significant problems with transferring assets, such as:

▲   Children can lose the money due to divorce or lawsuits. Remember, it doesn't take bad people to do bad things. Children may be tempted to spend the money in a financial crisis by subconsciously thinking they will inherit it any way, so why not use it now when they really need it? Then when you need long-term care, the money simply isn't there anymore.

▲   We tend to judge ourselves by what we have, either consciously or unconsciously. Once we have turned our assets over to someone else, either a child or a trust, we have lost control of them. We may not enjoy the feeling of not being able to access our assets ever again.

▲ Transferring assets and using government money means using our own money as taxpayers. In New York, for example, a minimum of 50% of county taxes goes to the Medicaid program, and some counties pay 75%. Medicaid in New York is running about $30 billion annually. A really shocking equation that most New Yorkers don't realize is that two out of every ten Medicaid recipients spend $8 out of every $10 of Medicaid benefits. The two recipients spending most of the money are spending it for long-term care. Seventy-five percent of the remaining eight recipients who are left with the $2 are *children*.

Let's take this picture national: One-fourth of the Medicaid budget in the United States is being spent on nursing home care.[2] Two-thirds of nursing home patients are on Medicaid.[3] The impact of people who have transferred assets to qualify for Medicaid is hurting all of us as taxpayers.

Transferring assets has been a safety net in the past to prevent losing a lifetime of hard-earned savings, but it hasn't been a *dignified* safety net, due to losing control of assets and thereby losing financial independence. Long-term care insurance provides the dignified safety net, and particularly the Partnership policies that now make that possible for middle-income Americans.

A few points you may be wondering about with the Partnership policies:

Portability—If you move to another state, the Partnership policy will pay, and the benefits will accumulate toward your asset protection threshold. However, to qualify for Medicaid and take advantage of the asset protection offered by the Partnership policies when your benefits run out, you must move back to the state in which you bought your Partnership policy and re-establish residence. Future legislation may make it possible for Partnership states to reciprocate the asset protection feature with each other, and Indiana and Connecticut are very close to accomplishing reciprocity.

Underwriting—You still must qualify for the Partnership policy medically just as you would for a standard long-term care insurance policy. The younger you are, the better the chance to qualify for a policy, and the lower the premiums. Pre-retirement ages (40's and 50's) are strongly encouraged to apply.

Arbitration—In some states, the Partnership policies have stronger mechanisms for claims appeals than standard long-term care policies. In those states, a rigorous consumer protection appeal process is in place for any Partnership policyholder who disagrees with a benefit determination.

Policy Continuance—If for any reason the Partnership program is discontinued either nationally or in its particular state, all policies will be honored and appropriate benefits paid by the insurance company that issued the policy.

Due to a change in the 1993 budget bill, Partnership states other than Connecticut, New York, Indiana, California and Iowa can offer asset protection only during the policyholder's lifetime. At death, the state is required to seek estate recovery for Medicaid's payment. This unfortunate legislation slowed development of Partnership programs in other states, but Illinois and Washington are pushing ahead by allowing certain transfers during a person's lifetime as a reward for purchasing a Partnership policy. Massachusetts offers another variation: Medicaid guidelines have to be met as usual so there is no up-front asset protection, but exempt assets in the eligibility process, such as a home, are also exempt from the estate recovery process at death.

Interested in finding out about your state's position on the Partnership program? Just call the Partnership office for the states listed on the next page. For other states, contact your congressional representatives and senators, your insurance department, Agency on Aging, or your Medicaid department (see **Who to Call for Help**, p. 225). Even if your state isn't participating in the program at this time, your phone call as an interested person can stimulate your state's legislators to become a participant.

State and National Partnership Offices

California 800-227-3445 www.dhs.ca.gov/cpltc	Iowa 515-281-6867
Connecticut 860-418-6318 www.opm.state.ct.us/pdpd4/ ltc/home.htm	New York 518-473-8083 www.nyspltc.org
Illinois 800-252-8966 (in IL only) 217-785-9021	Washington 360-407-0383
Indiana 800-452-4800 (in IN only) 317-233-3475 www.state.in.us/fssa/iltcp/ index.html	National 301-405-2532

Chapter 5

The Medicaid Benefit for Long-Term Care

〜〜〜〜〜〜〜〜〜〜〜〜〜〜〜〜〜〜〜〜〜〜〜〜〜〜

Medicaid is the public welfare program for the indigent jointly funded by federal, state and, in some states, local governments. Medicaid's huge growth in recent years is for "aged, blind and disabled" recipients. These people make up just over a third of the people entitled to Medicaid benefits, but they consume almost three-fourths of the benefit dollars. The driving force behind this inequity is nursing home costs for the elderly. A fourth of Medicaid funds were for nursing home costs in 1998.[1]

The Problem

The aging population combined with the escalating cost of long-term care and loopholes in Medicaid eligibility laws have encouraged a growing number of older Americans to transfer assets to capture public funding for nursing home expenses. However, shrinking tax dollars caused by the severe decline in the ratio of workers to Social Security beneficiaries, due to the aging population, have caused dire financial straits for the Medicaid program just as it has for Medicare. There have been several attempts to actually criminalize asset transfers either for the person who is seeking Medicaid benefits or for the advisor who paved the way. These attempts to date have been unsuccessful, but many legislators believe the issue is too important to let it drop. The purpose of legislation of this nature is to restore Medicaid's original purpose—to help poor people.

The Medicaid nursing home benefit is intended for people with low income and very low assets. This means that an applicant has to meet both income and asset criteria to qualify for Medicaid benefits.

Income Eligibility Criteria

States are able to choose one of two methods to determine income eligibility:

1) The most drastic method allows the nursing home spouse to have income up to three times the Supplemental Security Income (SSI) amount, or $1,590 for 2001. Because that amount is so low compared to the cost of nursing home care ($3,500-$5,000 a month nationwide), the 1993 budget bill made a way to help people with low assets and income that exceeds this low monthly allowance but is not enough to pay privately.

   These people can assign their income to a "Miller trust," also called a "qualified income trust," which is a special irrevocable trust designed just for the purpose of helping someone in a cap state whose assets qualify for Medicaid, but income is greater than the cap but not enough to pay privately.

   Here's how it works: The individual is allowed to keep a personal-needs allowance, usually $30 a month. All of the remaining income can be assigned to the trust or just the amount that exceeds the cap plus a little extra just to be safe.

For example, if someone has $1,800 a month in income, which exceeds the $1,590 cap by $210, it would be wise to put at least $250 into the Miller trust in case of income fluctuations due to interest rates, etc. The individual's income still goes to the nursing home every month, but it will be a combination of the income retained by the individual and a monthly payment from the Miller trust, unless the individual assigned all of his or her income to the trust. In that case, the trust will make a single payment to the nursing home each month. Medicaid then makes up the difference between the individual's income and the Medicaid rate for the nursing home, which varies by facility.

The state is entitled to any excess income that has accumulated in the trust at the death of the applicant to pay Medicaid back for nursing home expenses Medicaid paid while the person was alive.

The 19 states that work this way are called "income cap" states and they are: Alabama, Alaska, Arizona, Arkansas, Colorado, Delaware, Florida, Idaho, Iowa, Louisiana, Mississippi, Nevada, New Mexico, Oklahoma, Oregon, South Carolina, South Dakota, Texas, and Wyoming.

2) The remaining states allow the applicant to have income up to the cost of care, usually the Medicaid rate for the nursing home. This amount—about $2,500-$3,500 for

most states, but can run as high as $7,000 a month or so for "high cost areas" like metropolitan New York City-varies by facility but there is a maximum for each state. The Medicaid rate is lower than the private pay rate in most states, but a few states allow applicants to have income up to the private pay cost of nursing home care. Check with your Medicaid department for your specific state information. (See **Who to Call for Help** on page 225.)

How is income determined? First, "the name on the check" rule applies. Social Security or pension income is easily attributable. Trust or investment income that is directed jointly to a married couple is divided 50/50. Starting with the gross monthly income for the Medicaid applicant, all individuals are allowed to keep a "personal needs" allowance—about $1 a day, or $30 a month in most states—but it can be as high as $75 a month, as in Alaska and Arizona. In non-cap states, there are a few allowable deductions to get the income down to the Medicaid qualifying level.

▲ health insurance premium, such as a Medicare supplement or retiree health premium, usually in the range of $100 a month

▲ any medical expense not reimbursed by Medicaid or any other source (for example, a particular prescription that Medicaid doesn't cover)

▲ income needed for the spouse at home, subject to a range established by Medicaid ($1,407* minimum—$2,175 maximum a month for the period 7/1/00–6/30/01)   *This amount changes each July.

For example, Mr. Jones has $2,000 a month of his own income. After subtracting $30 for the personal needs allowance, $100 for a Medicare supplement premium, and $50 for his monthly prescriptions that aren't paid by any other source, he is left with $1,820. Mrs. Jones has $800 a month of her own Social Security income and a small pension. This means that Mr. Jones can transfer $607 of his income to her to bring her up to $1,407,* the minimum monthly Medicaid allowance for the spouse at home. This gets his income down to $1,213, which easily qualifies him for Medicaid to pay his nursing home bill.

His income of $1,213 then goes to the nursing home. Let's say that the Medicaid rate for that nursing home is $87 per day, or $2,700 a month. Medicaid will then make up the difference between his income and the Medicaid rate and will pay the nursing home $1,487 a month on his behalf. ($2,700-$1,213).

You're wondering how the spouse at home can receive more than the minimum monthly income allowance. Some states just use the maximum and allow the spouse at home to keep that much income if the couple has that much income between them. The states that allow the maximum income allowance for the spouse at home are Alaska, Arizona, California, Georgia, Hawaii, Illinois, Iowa, Kentucky, Louisiana, Mississippi, Nebraska, New York, North Dakota, Oklahoma, Texas, Wisconsin and Wyoming, and the District of Columbia.

Other states require the spouse at home to justify the need for more income than the minimum of $1,407 per month. The justification process is based on whether or not there are "shelter costs" such as rent, a mortgage payment, homeowners insurance,

*This amount changes each July.

property taxes, a condominium maintenance fee, utilities, etc. If these shelter costs exceed a monthly amount called the "excess shelter allowance" ($422 for 2000*) the spouse at home can keep additional income. Here's how it works:

The difference between the total shelter costs ($900 a month, for example) and the Excess Shelter Allowance ($422) is added to the $1,407and this becomes the monthly allowance for the spouse in this example:

$ 900	Total monthly "shelter" costs
− $ 422	Excess Shelter Allowance
$ 478	Additional spousal income allowable
+ $1,407	Minimum monthly spousal income allowance
$1,885	Total monthly spousal income allowance

Some states are allowing couples to retain more resources to generate the above allowable monthly income. This is called the "asset first" or "resource first" rule. Sometimes this is construed as a couple being able to retain a large amount of resources by putting them in very low interest-bearing accounts, such as certificates of deposits or bank savings accounts. In 1993 an Iowa judge ruled against this method and required the couple to purchase a single premium life annuity that would yield the necessary income for the life of the spouse at home.[2] Using this method may not make it possible to pass resources on to heirs if the spouse meets or exceeds life expectancy as all of the money would be paid out during the spouse's lifetime.

*This amount changes each July.

Conversely, some states, like Ohio and New York, practice the "income first" rule, which means the state won't allow a couple to retain resources to generate income for the spouse until the nursing home spouse has shifted all possible income to the spouse at home.[3] Then if the spouse's income is still below the minimum, the state will allow additional income from retained resources. The "income first" rule keeps the amount of resources retained for this purpose as small as possible.

Asset Eligibility Criteria

Applicants for Medicaid also have to meet stringent asset criteria as well as income criteria. Generally, people with "countable" assets of about $2,000 ($3,000-$4,000 if both spouses need nursing home care) can qualify. (This amount varies slightly by state.) Assets do not include the house and car if you have a spouse still living in the house and using the car. The house and car still won't count for a single person if that person has a reasonable hope of getting better and going home. If the single person is not likely to return home, usually for six months, then the state can require the house to be sold.

"Countable assets" include anything that is available as a resource to you. In other words, anything that you can take money out of, even if you have to pay surrender charges (for example, an annuity that is only a couple of years old) or sell at a loss (for example, stock or property outside your primary residence). Here's a partial list of assets that count:

▲ cash (checking and savings accounts)
▲ certificates of deposit (CDs)
▲ money market accounts

- mutual funds
- stocks
- bonds
- deferred annuities
- property outside the home*
- cash value in life insurance for policies with a face value of $1,500 or more**
- revocable trust (a living trust, for example)
- burial trusts beyond a minimum amount, unless they are irrevocable**
- retirement accounts like 401(k), Keoghs, SEPTS, IRA plans, etc.

The rule of thumb is, if you can access the principal, it counts as an asset for Medicaid purposes.

If you are married, you can't just put everything in your spouse's name. When you apply for Medicaid to pay nursing home expenses, all countable assets (see list above) are considered, regardless of whose name the assets are in—husband's or wife's—and includes a spouse's retirement account with rare exception. This is true even if you and your spouse have a prenuptial agreement. Many states will not honor a divorce agreement if the state believes the purpose of the divorce is solely to establish Medicaid eligibility for long-term care.

---

*Some states won't count property outside the home as an asset if rented, but those states usually count the rental income toward the income eligibility requirements. Also, income-producing property outside the home, such as a business location or a working ranch or farm, usually is not counted.

**Varies by state.

The minimum asset amount for the spouse at home is $17,400 for 2001, which means if one-half of the assets are less than the minimum, the spouse at home is allowed to keep the minimum.

Total assets are divided equally between you and your spouse. The spouse applying for Medicaid spends his or her half down to the state's asset requirement (usually $2,000) and the spouse at home can keep a maximum of $87,000 for 2001. In most states, the only way the spouse at home receives the maximum is if one-half of the assets is equal to or exceeds the maximum. Otherwise, the spouse at home receives 50% of the assets.

Here's how it works:

Example #1: $200,000 in countable assets: One-half is $100,000, which exceeds the maximum. The spouse at home keeps $87,000.

Example #2: $80,000 in countable assets: One-half is $40,000, which does not equal or exceed the maximum. The spouse at home keeps $40,000.

Example #3: $20,000 in countable assets. One-half is $10,000, which is less than the minimum. The spouse at home keeps $17,400.

Some states are more liberal and allow the spouse at home to keep the maximum of $87,000 as long as the couple has that much in assets. Those states are Alaska, California, Colorado, Florida, Georgia, Hawaii, Illinois, Kentucky, Louisiana, Maine, Massachusetts, Mississippi, North Dakota, Vermont, Wyoming, and the District of Columbia. A few other states have minimums in between:

Alabama	$25,000	New York	$74,820
Delaware	$25,000	Oklahoma	$25,000
Idaho	$17,400	South Carolina	$66,480
Iowa	$24,000	South Dakota	$20,000
Minnesota	$24,607	Washington	$87,000
New Mexico	$31,290	Wisconsin	$50,000

In those states, the spouse at home is allowed to keep the amount shown as long as the couple has that much in assets.

Transferring Assets—The Myth

Surely the simple solution to all this is to just give assets to children or place them in a trust—perhaps for a favorite charity. That way the nursing home doesn't get your hard-earned assets, and you get something back for all those years of paying taxes. The really important thing is to get the house out of your name, so Medicaid and/or the nursing home can't get it.

Between the 1993 budget bill (OBRA '93) and the 1996 and 1997 health care reform, Congress thinks these are very bad ideas. Here's why:

When someone in a nursing home applies for Medicaid to pay nursing home expenses, Medicaid "looks back" 36 months (30 months in California) to see if a transfer has occurred, for example, to children.* The look-back period is 60 months for transfers to an irrevocable trust; that is, a trust set up so that the

---

*If the application is made before being admitted to a nursing home, the look-back period is counted back from the date of nursing home admission, not from the date of application.

applicant cannot receive any income or principal from it. If a transfer has occurred during that time, the applicant is ineligible for Medicaid benefits for the number of months equal to the amount of the transfer divided by the state's average monthly cost of nursing home care. The Medicaid office in your state can tell you your state's average cost of care (see **Who to Call for Help**, p. 225) Prior to 10/1/93, the longest an applicant would have to wait for Medicaid benefits after a transfer was 30 months, but OBRA '93 eliminated the cap. Now the "period of ineligibility" for Medicaid benefits depends on the amount of the transfer.

For example, a $300,000 transfer divided by a $3,500 average monthly cost for nursing home care equals 85.7 months (7 years) of ineligibility.

Transfers can be outright gifts or done in more subtle ways:

▲ Transferring $10,000 per year ($20,000 if you are married) to your children and grandchildren to stay within the federal gift-tax exclusion.

▲ Setting up a joint checking account with a son or daughter, then removing the parent's name from the account.

▲ Putting a home in the name of a son or daughter or other family member or friend.

▲ Transferring assets into an immediate annuity, which changes the assets into income. Medicaid compares the amount of the annuity with your life expectancy. Any projected payout that exceeds life expectancy is treated as a transfer and will trigger a period of ineligibility.

▲ Transferring assets into an immediate annuity and producing a monthly income for the spouse at home, also known as "the community spouse." Note: a February 28, 2000, Ohio case ruled such a transfer was improper and denied Medicaid benefits for the appropriate penalty period.[4]

▲ Transferring assets into a trust to fund a college education for a grandchild.

▲ Setting up a trust that will benefit a charity after your death, so you can receive the income while you are alive.

▲ Setting up a trust that will benefit a charity with regular income before your death, then the principal will go to a family member when you die.

▲ Donating to a "pooled-income fund"—similar to a mutual fund operated by a charity for smaller investors to reap the tax benefits of charitable giving without having to invest large amounts.

All of these methods can count as a transfer of assets and trigger a penalty period, which means a period of ineligibility for Medicaid benefits. The motive of the transfer has no bearing on this process. There are professionals (attorneys, accountants, financial planners, etc.) who have helped people make transfers around the look-back period (i.e., 37 months before applying for Medicaid or 61 months if trusts are used). The advisor might

Why Transferring Assets Can Be a Bad Idea

Divorce	Half your assets go to buy your favorite son-in-law or daughter-in-law a red BMW!
Financial Difficulties	Every family has financial down times. Your daughter is thinking "I'm going to inherit the money anyway . . ."
Mis-Use of Funds	It looked like the best stock pick of the century.
Lawsuit	Your son is sued and your assets—now his assets as far as the court is concerned—are attached.
College Financial Aid	Your grandson no longer qualifies for financial aid because you shifted your assets to his father.
Cost-Basis	You paid $10 a share for the stock you just gave your daughter. It is now worth $100 a share. She sells the stock and owes tax on the gain of $90 per share . . . the tax bill may be more than a lifetime of long-term care insurance premium for you!
Early Death of Adult Child	The unthinkable happens—your son or daughter predeceases you. Your assets are now in the hands of the in-laws.
Adverse Tax Consequences	Interest earned on the transferred assets are taxable income to your children and amounts above $10,000 transferred in any one calendar year use up part of your lifetime estate and gift tax exemption ($675,000 in 2001). Some states have separate gift taxes from federal gift taxes.

A good long-term care insurance policy can mean you don't have to worry about these problems!

suggest keeping enough assets to pay privately during the look-back period, in case the person needs nursing home care before the lookback period has expired. Then the person could apply for Medicaid after the lookback period had expired. This is sometimes called the "half-a-loaf" theory—transfer half of your assets and keep half of your assets to pay privately during the 36 or 60 month lookback period.

Note: Setting up a special trust for a disabled dependent can be accomplished in certain instances if you designate that the principal will revert to the state at the death of the disabled dependent. You should seek advice from an elder law attorney for help with this and any type of trust. Visit the National Academy of Elder Law Attorneys at www.naela.org for a list of elder law attorneys in your area.

Estate Recovery

People who qualify for Medicaid by transferring assets successfully around the lookback period or whose assets are tied up in their home which is a non-countable asset face yet another huge hurdle. OBRA '93 requires states to recover from the estate of anyone who receives Medicaid benefits at the death of the second spouse. Some states include recovery from the spouse's estate of any assets that the Medicaid recipient at the time of death conveyed to the spouse "through joint tenancy, tenancy in common, survivorship, life estate, living trust, or other arrangement" (*North Dakota Dept. of Human Services v. Thompson,* December 22, 1998).[5] Another North Dakota case said all assets in which the Medicaid recipient once held an interest are subject to estate recovery, even if those assets had not been formally conveyed.[6]

A recent development in estate recovery is that, effective January 24, 2000, the U.S. Health Care Financing Administration (the organization that oversees Medicare and Medicaid) ruled that a state has the option to recover Medicaid expenditures from the surviving beneficiary of an annuity that was owned by a Medicaid nursing home patient. However, recovery cannot be made as long as a surviving spouse or minor or disabled child is alive.[7]

The recovery process also includes in most states the right to place a lien on your home in the amount of Medicaid payments made on your behalf for your care. When the property is sold or title is transferred, the lien must be paid. States have the right to place a lien on even a "life estate," which is simply a legal interest you keep in your home after you have transferred the deed to someone else. And if you give your house away outright, you lose the capital gains exclusion.

Your children (or to whomever you give the house) could take advantage of the capital gains exclusion, but only if they live in the house at least two of the last five years before the house is sold. Giving your house to your kids and continuing to live in it can mean your children wind up paying a steep capital gains tax when the house is sold if they don't adhere to the capital gains exclusion rules of living in the house the appropriate time before its sale.

"More than half the states place liens on homes to protect their interest," according to *Kiplinger's Personal Finance Magazine.*[8] The lien is not enforceable, however, until the death of the second spouse, even if he or she does not live in the house, and Medicaid must notify your family in advance that a lien is being placed.

Liens also cannot be enforced if:

▲   There is a child under age 21, or who is blind or disabled, whether or not the child lives in the house.

▲   There is a brother or sister with a joint ownership for the year immediately prior to the nursing home admission, but only if he or she lived in the house continuously since that date.

▲   There is a non-disabled adult child who had lived in the house two or more years prior to the parent's admission to a nursing home, and who had provided care that delayed admission, but the child must have lived in the house continuously since then.

An excellent publication, entitled *Questions and Answers on Medicaid Estate Recovery for Long-Term Care Under OBRA '93*, is available free from AARP by writing the Public Policy Institute, 601 "E" Street, NW, Washington, DC 20049, or you can access it online at http://research.aarp.org.

The Bigger Problem—The Criminal Side Revisited

A variety of legislative attempts to criminalize asset transfers for the sole purpose of qualifying for Medicaid has put a huge chill on the practice of "Medicaid planning," the process of impoverishing oneself on paper to qualify for Medicaid's nursing home benefit. The Balanced Budget Act of 1997 had this to say about Medicaid planning:

Whoever . . . for a fee knowingly and willfully counsels or assists an individual to dispose of assets (including by any transfer in trust) in order for an individual to become eligible for medical assistance (Medicaid), if disposing of the assets results in the imposition of a period of ineligibility for such assistance . . . shall . . . be guilty of a criminal offense.

Due to the efforts primarily of the New York State Bar Association, this legislation was declared unenforceable in 1998 by Attorney General Janet Reno. A little publicized comment in her letter on the subject to [then] Speaker of the House Newt Gingrich was that she would be glad to help Congress write something that would be enforceable. An injunction against the law was granted later in the year by New York Judge Thomas McElvoy in September 1998, who also ruled that it was unconstitutional. Attorney General Reno then filed a notice of appeal on December 18, 1998, which was the necessary step to protect the Justice Department's right to appeal the injunction.

Prior to the Balanced Budget Act's attempt, the Health Insurance Accountability and Portability Act of 1996 made it a criminal offense, effective January 1, 1997, for the person who transfers the assets, not the person's legal or financial advisor. That law quickly earned the name, "The Granny Goes to Jail Law." The National Association of Elder Law Attorneys raised a huge outcry and lobbied furiously to get it repealed, saying it just wasn't fair to send Grandma to jail, and the law should be dismissed. Congress agreed only partially with their case and eliminated the part about Grandma going to jail and replaced it with the above language in the Balanced Budget Act that seeks to punish the professional who charges a fee to help someone transfer assets to qualify for Medicaid.

The present status is that the Justice Department withdrew the December 1998 notice of appeal mentioned above in March

1999. However, these attempts show an increasing interest to restrict access to Medicaid to the truly needy.

Why does such a strong interest exist to close the loopholes for Medicaid planning?

Because there aren't enough tax dollars to pay for a national long-term care plan, and that's the direction this program is taking when you consider that Medicaid pays 46% of nursing home costs and two-thirds of all nursing home patients are Medicaid recipients.[9] 44 cents of every Federal income tax dollar in the U.S. goes to pay for entitlements (mainly, Social Security, Medicare and Medicaid), and this is only a prelude *before* the baby boomers start applying for Medicaid nursing home benefits![10] In view of these facts, it is reasonable to expect that legislative activity to curtail Medicaid planning will continue.

The Biggest Problem

All of the above are problems, but the biggest problem is that by giving your assets away, you lose access to them, and you lose the one thing that matters most—**your independence and control.** That's why you gave the assets away to start with—to keep from losing them to a nursing home—and now for one or more of the above reasons, you've lost them anyway.

Here's what it means to be a Medicaid patient in most states:

    You can't get into strictly private-pay facilities that don't accept Medicaid patients.

▲ Medicaid pays very little for home health care, so being on Medicaid in most states means being in a nursing home. States can get permission to pay some Medicaid benefits in assisted living facilities like for personal care and homemaker services that are usually not covered by the state's regular Medicaid program, but *Medicaid does not pay the room and board charge in assisted living facilities,* and that's the bulk of the charge.

▲ Medicaid pays less than private-pay rates in most states, so the waiting lists are long for Medicaid patients.

▲ You have to go wherever there is a bed, which could be hours away from your family.

▲ If the facility doesn't accept Medicaid and you run out of your own money, you can be required to move to a facility that accepts Medicaid, and that's a hard situation for families to deal with.*

▲ Nursing homes that operate with predominantly Medicaid patients don't have as much funding as private-pay facilities to upgrade services, furnishings, etc.

▲ You simply don't have as many choices as a private-pay patient—a private room, for example, is not allowed—because as a Medicaid patient, you aren't paying the bill.

*On March 25, 1999, President Clinton signed into law the Nursing Home Resident Protection Act of 1999 which means that nursing homes that voluntarily drop out of Medicaid can refuse to admit new Medicaid patients, but they can't force Medicaid patients already in residence to leave. This does not, however, prevent nursing homes from dropping out of Medicaid altogether and being totally private-pay facilities. To prevent surprises, this law requires private-pay facilities to notify patients upon admission that they will have to leave if they run out of their own money and need to apply for Medicaid.

As Joan Gruber, a Dallas financial planner who works mainly with families of the elderly, says, "No one would voluntarily set themselves up for Medicaid if they understood what it's like."[11] And a spokesperson for the American Association of Homes and Services for the Aging (which represents nonprofit nursing homes) says, "The more money you have, the more options you will have in terms of paying for care at home or for assisted living. I would never recommend that someone who has money get rid of it to go on Medicaid."[12]

Long-Term Care Insurance—A Better Way

The message sent by the federal government is clear: Medicaid is a program for poor people and is not to be used by middle- and upper-income Americans. Many reliable publications such as Suze Orman's **The 9 Steps to Financial Freedom** (Crown, 1997), Dave Ramsey's **Financial Peace** (Viking, 1997) and *Fortune* magazine encourage people to buy long-term care insurance instead of relying on Medicaid. Well-known financial advisor Jane Bryant Quinn in *The Washington Post* (October 10, 1996) says that Medicaid planning is unethical and she, too, encourages people to buy long-term care insurance instead of relying on Medicaid to pay nursing home bills:

The ethical elderly do indeed use their money to pay their own nursing home bills. But growing numbers just say no—egged on by their adult children who don't want to see their inheritance slip away. Medicaid's quality may decline, if taxpayers resent the cost. Long-term care insurance is looking like the better choice.

Beware of anyone who advises you to transfer assets to artificially impoverish yourself so that Medicaid will pay for your nursing home expenses—not only is this kind of action morally and ethically questionable, it can result in serious legal and financial consequences. *In many cases the tax ramifications of transferring your cost-basis for your assets and/or your home cost far more than a lifetime of premium for a long-term care policy!*

Ultimately, the transfer may prove to be ineffective if there are no Medicaid beds available when you need one. Even today, some communities have year-long waiting lists for Medicaid beds!

The primary reason people are purchasing long-term care insurance policies is to maintain choice, and consequently, **independence.** (See **Long-Term Care and Your Financial Security.**)

If you are the type of person who enjoys being in control, a long-term care insurance policy may be the only thing that makes it possible for you to stay in control by guaranteeing that you will have purchasing power—and consequently decision-making power—when you need long-term care, which means choices other than a nursing home—home health care, adult day care, and the beautiful private-pay assisted living facilities that represent the fastest growing form of long-term care.

If a nursing home patient thinks he or she will qualify for Medicaid eventually, it is recommended that an application be made to Medicaid upon admission to the nursing home so a financial assessment can be made at that time. Applicants who wait until assets are spent down to the qualifying level of $2,000 must furnish financial information back to the admission date, and that is not always easy to do.

If you are interested in applying for Medicaid to pay your nursing home expenses, contact your local Medicaid office, which is usually listed in the state government section in the blue pages of your telephone book or see **Who to Call for Help** on p. 225 for state Medicaid offices. Or you may call your state's Agency on Aging and ask that office to tell you the telephone number to call for Medicaid information.

Chapter 6

Alternatives for Financing Long-Term Care

〜〜〜〜〜〜〜〜〜〜〜〜〜〜〜〜〜〜〜〜〜〜〜〜〜〜〜〜〜〜〜

Other ways people consider financing long-term care are through accelerated death riders to life insurance policies, viatical or life settlements, life/long-term care policies, annuity/long-term care policies and reverse mortgages. An overview of each of these five options is presented as additional information for the long-term care planning process.

Accelerated Death Benefits

An alternative to purchasing a long-term care insurance policy as described in the preceding section is to purchase a life insurance policy that will provide cash advances against all or a portion of the death benefit to pay for long-term care expenses while the insured is still living. Because the death benefit can be paid out early, this form of long-term care payment as a part of a life insurance policy is commonly referred to as an accelerated death benefit, but you also may hear it referred to as a "living needs" benefit or "rider." Early versions only paid if the policyholder suffered from a terminal illness, and that is still the most common triggering event. Today about 20% of these policies make the benefit available for chronically ill people as well. Two-thirds of these pay only for permanent confinement in a nursing home, but some pay also for home and community-based care, like assisted living, and a handful pay only for home care.[1]

The accelerated death benefit is an alternative to traditional LTC insurance policies for some people because this provision can be added to a life insurance policy for little or no cost. It also can help someone who cannot qualify for a traditional LTC policy at an older age if the benefit was included in the policyholder's life insurance at time of purchase, as is the case with many younger purchasers of life insurance today. As of 1997, these types of policies represented 7% of total LTC policies sold and had enjoyed an average annual growth rate of 76% since 1988.[2]

Typically, monthly benefits for long-term care will equal 2% of the face value of the policy for nursing home care and 1% for home health care. For example, if the face value of the policy is $150,000, the nursing home benefit would be $3,000 a month and the home care benefit would be $1,500. Some policies do not reduce the payout for home care.

Newer policies tend to be reimbursement policies, which means they will pay actual charges up to the available benefit equal to 2% of face value. Older policies were commonly indemnity plans, which paid out the 2% amount, regardless of charge. The Health Insurance Portability and Accountability Act of 1996 (HIPAA) is primarily responsible for this change (see *Recent Health Care Reform* on p. 19 for a list of provisions). Benefit payments in excess of $190 per day in 2000 (or the monthly equivalent) that exceed the actual cost of care will be taxed as income, so most long-term care insurance policies of all types stick with paying the actual charges to help the policyholder avoid a precarious tax situation.

The pitfalls? Even at 2% of the face value for all benefits, the monthly benefit payments are likely to be lower and durations of coverage shorter than under freestanding LTC insurance products, because many people do not have life insurance policies with large face amounts. So if the life insurance policy has a face value of $100,000, the monthly benefit would be $2,000. In metropolitan areas, that benefit amount would only pick up about half the cost of either a nursing home or daily eight-hour shifts of home health care. If the policy advanced the entire face amount, in this example, the benefit duration would be only about four years.

Other pitfalls are that some policies still pay a lower benefit for home health care. An especially serious problem is that inflation may not be addressed. Also, if the primary need is for life insurance, utilizing the death benefit for long-term care expenses defeats the purpose of the insurance by leaving the survivors with little or no death benefit after the insured is deceased. However, the 1996 health care legislation provided much needed clarification that accelerated death benefits will be treated as if they were the proceeds payable on account of death—that is, income-tax free—if the benefits meet the criteria of HIPAA. Non-qualified versions are being sold, however, so check carefully to see if the sales brochures, sample policies, etc., have notification on the front that the policy is tax-qualified. Tax-qualified pieces are supposed to be clearly marked.

Since the cost to add an accelerated death benefit option to a life insurance policy is minimal with most policies, younger people may consider the rider a very good purchasing decision, similar to purchasing the right to buy a discounted freestanding LTC policy at older ages when purchasing a disability income policy.

Many employers have an accelerated death benefit provision in their group life insurance plans. Favorable tax treatment ensures that this interest will continue to grow rapidly.

Traditional Viatical Settlements

Taking its name from "viaticum"— the supplies needed to perform last rites that were routinely sent into battle with Roman soldiers (who commonly weren't expected to return)—a traditional viatical settlement allows a terminally ill individual to "sell" a life insurance policy to a third party. The core idea is that the proceeds from the sale of the policy would provide "financial supplies" for the final journey of death. The reality is that the third party (the viatical company) pays the terminally ill person a percentage of the death benefit and becomes the owner and beneficiary of the life insurance policy and takes over the premium payments. The terminally ill person gets funds to live on during the very costly time before death, and the third party receives the full death benefit after the person dies.

"Terminally ill" for a viatical company can be anyone with a life expectancy of five years or less, but typically is 2–3 years.

The amount paid for the policy is based on the life expectancy of the insured and is influenced by other factors such as:

▲   **The Capitalization of the Viatical Company**—Most viatical companies do not bear the risk of the viatical arrangement of paying out a discounted death benefit and waiting until the person dies to collect the entire death amount. Rather, most viaticals are brokers that bring together investors and terminally ill people. At least one insurance company acts as a viatical settlement provider and bears the risk of buying life insurance policies.

▲ **Case Diversification of the Viatical Company**—The viatical business started with AIDS patients. Viatical companies that have continued to purchase mainly the life insurance policies of AIDS patients are not doing well because technology has drastically extended the lives of AIDS patients. A successful viatical company has a good mix of terminal conditions, like cancer and heart-related conditions, as well as late-stage conditions, such as Alzheimer's.

▲ **Rating of the Insurance Company**—Viatical companies make a lower payment if the insurance company has a rating of B+ or lower according to the A.M. Best company, the largest third-party rating service for insurance companies. Why? Because if the lower-rated company goes out of business, the viatical company gets stuck with a policy on which it probably can't collect.

▲ **Waiver of Premium Status**—If the premium of the policy is waived due to a provision that waives the premium because the policyholder is disabled, the viatical company will have more money available since it won't have to assume premium payments.

▲ **Investor Mix**—Investors who are short-term, high-return speculative investors demand a higher interest rate for their investment dollars which will lower the amount available to pay out in discounted death benefits.

Viatical companies buy all kinds of life insurance policies: term, whole life, universal life, and group life. A viatical settlement can be a "knight in shining armor" for an employee who is too sick to work and must convert the group life policy to an individual policy in order to keep it. The premium for a converted policy can be steep, and many employees aren't prepared to pay a high premium. A viatical company can purchase the policy and pick up the premium.

The Viatical Settlement Process

The terminally ill person submits an application. The viatical company confirms the insurance policy with the insurance company and obtains medical records to determine the life expectancy of the applicant. There is no application fee.

If the viatical company decides to purchase the policy, the minimum payment to the insured based on life expectancy may follow this table which represents minimum guidelines suggested by the National Association of Insurance Commissioners:

Life Expectancy of Insured	% of Net Death Benefit* Paid
1–6 months	80%
6–12 months	70%
12–18 months	65%
18–24 months	60%
24 +	50%

* Payment is based on net death benefit, not face value of the policy. Net death benefit means the actual benefit payable at death, which may have been reduced by policy loans or withdrawals.

These percentages can be higher based on criteria listed at the beginning of this section and can be 5% lower than these guidelines if the insurance company is rated B+ or lower. In 1999, a "reasonableness standard" was added as an alternative to the table of minimum payments. Your insurance department can explain further about this alternative as criteria is jointly developed using data supplied annually by viatical settlement providers and reasonableness criteria provided by the National Association of Insurance Commissioners.

A large viatical company reports that forty percent of applications are approved. Sixty percent are declined because life expectancy is beyond five years, which means the payment offer is usually low and not attractive to the applicant.

There is a 15-day rescission period, which means the applicant can change his or her mind for any reason and resume ownership of the policy. One viatical company's practice is to reinstate the original beneficiary if the original owner dies within the 15-day rescission period, although there is no requirement for the viatical company to do so.

Policies of all sizes are viaticated. One company's range is $5,000–$6,000,000, with an average of $102,000 in death benefit.

Most states (including most of the larger ones) have adopted viatical settlement legislation, so most of the population in the United States is covered by consumer protection regulation for viatical settlements.

The Health Insurance Portability and Accountability Act of 1996 (HIPAA) enables viatical settlements to be tax-free for terminal individuals with a two-year or less life expectancy or for chronically ill individuals. Note: It is the health care practitioner (physician, nurse, or social worker) that determines the tax status. The viatical company may think life expectancy is three years, but if the health care practitioner thinks two, then the discounted death benefit paid out will be tax-free because the IRS goes by the health care practitioner's certification. Also, the IRS doesn't look back. If the individual exceeds life expectancy, the IRS won't challenge the tax-free benefit status.

To receive the settlement tax-free, however, the viator must do business with a viatical company that is licensed in the states that require licensing or adheres to the NAIC guidelines for payment (described on the preceding page) in those states that do not require licensing. The NAIC also has specific consumer disclosure requirements, so that viators understand all of the ramifications of the viatical settlement.

Several states, such as California and New York, have also made viatical funds free of state income taxes.

Viatical Settlements vs. Accelerated Death Benefits

▲   The ability to accelerate the death benefit, that is, to collect a portion of the death benefit while still living for chronically ill individuals, not just terminally ill, is only available on a small percentage of life insurance policies in force. (A little over three million policies had been sold with a chronically-ill trigger benefit as of the end of 1997, the majority of which will only accelerate the death benefit if you are permanently confined to a nursing home. Less than 7% of these will pay for home and community care.)[3] Viatical companies, on the other hand, can purchase policies from any insurance company.

▲ The accelerated death benefit (ADB) policy may only pay out a portion, then apply a loan interest rate to the remaining death benefit, which means the beneficiaries won't get the entire remaining death benefit.

▲ Even though the health care reform legislation of 1996 allows the "terminally ill" requirement for an ADB to be up to 24 months, most ADB policies are six to 12 months, much shorter than a viatical settlement which runs up to five years.

▲ An ADB policy can lapse if premiums are not paid. The viatical settlement is a one-time procedure and all the money due the applicant is paid out all at one time. The terminally or chronically ill person no longer has to worry about paying premium and keeping a policy in force.

Some ADB policies may have a payout that is less than 50% of the death benefit, and a little over half of them are capped at 50%. The payout on a traditional viatical settlement is usually 50%-80% but typically is higher than an ADB policy that is capped at 50%. There is no maximum age at which a viatical settlement can occur. In fact, viatical arrangements are now available to individuals aged 70+ with no medical underwriting (see next section, *Life Settlements*)

Viatical Settlements vs. Long-Term Care Insurance

▲ For people without long-term care insurance, a viatical settlement can provide a solution to immediate cash needs. A small portion of the settlement could also be used to purchase a long-term care policy for the surviving partner.

▲ Viatical settlements represent a great alternative to Medicaid planning for the person who is unable to qualify for long-term care insurance due to problems with health or affordability.

▲ LTC insurance stretches the money out vs. paying the full cost of long-term care services with a lump-sum viatical settlement, which can disappear quickly, especially with the temptation to spend it on things other than the cost of care.

▲ Long-term care insurance can preserve the death benefit of the life insurance policy for family members.

▲ A long-term care insurance policy with an unlimited benefit period can pay benefits tax-free for an unlimited time period vs. a lump-sum viatical settlement that will run out.

Life Settlements

In addition to traditional viatical settlements as outlined above to help people who are chronically or terminally ill, a broad expansion of this idea, entitled a "life settlement," is available **for older people who are not ill**. These are just people who no longer need a death benefit because the original reason they bought life insurance doesn't exist anymore (for example, college tuition, change in estate size, sale of a business or divorce) or perhaps they can't afford the premium after retirement, a classic problem with term life insurance.

Today any male age 70 or older or any female age 74 or older who has life insurance (group, individual, term, whole life, universal life) can sell their policies to a life settlement company for their present value, an opportunity that can be a significant estate planning tool. Policies of almost any size can be purchased, from $5,000-$35,000,000, for example. This includes the policies held in irrevocable life insurance trusts, buy-sell agreements, and "key-man" policies. The proceeds from the policy sale are unrestricted, and high net worth individuals have the ability to use the funds for such options as:

▲ making cash gifts to family members
▲ purchasing a minority interest in a closely held business to reduce estate taxes
▲ facilitate the transfer of a business to the next generation
▲ funding the purchase of permanent life insurance that will insure a spouse to cover estate taxes
▲ paying long-term care expenses for someone who is uninsurable
▲ funding the purchase of long-term care insurance for a spouse
▲ making charitable gifts and funding planned giving techniques
▲ purchasing a business
▲ paying down debt
▲ investing the proceeds

As you can see, disposition of the funds is up to the imagination and simply represents a way to use life insurance while living. A few life settlement companies will even purchase a life insurance policy from someone as young as 65 if the life expectancy is in the 12 year range, which may be the case with certain health conditions.

Here is an example of using proceeds from a life settlement for long-term care:

> *An 80-year old gentleman, with some health concerns, had a $400,000 universal life insurance policy that had very little cash value. Making the premium payments was becoming a financial burden, and they were also concerned about long-term care for each of them. Unfortunately, he did not qualify for long-term care insurance because of his health problems. A life settlement gave him $175,000. The sale of this policy not only relieved this couple of the monthly premium payments but the life settlement funds enabled the client to purchase a long-term care policy for his wife, and also provided funds for his own long-term care needs.[4] Lifetime settlement payments incur tax liability to the original policyholder in two ways. First, the difference between the settlement payment and the cash surrender value is taxed as a capital gain. The difference between the total premiums paid (the tax basis) and the cash surrender value is taxed as ordinary income.[5]*

You should discuss your individual tax situation with a professional tax advisor.

Single Premium Life/Long-Term Care Policies

A growing number of consumers have expressed interest in a long-term care funding method in which a single premium is paid—i.e., a lump sum deposit—and that premium is guaranteed not to change. In standard LTC policies, there are very few companies with a one-time premium guaranteed not to change, and relatively few that have a limited payment option, such as 10-pay or 20-pay or "pay to age 65". Most policies require premiums to be paid for life, just like health insurance, and the premium can be increased in the future if it is increased on an entire classification of policyholders.

Increasingly, the consumer interested in the lump sum, paid-up approach says, "I want to pay one time, and if I don't use the policy, I want my money to be passed on to my [children, grandchildren, church, charity, etc]." The policy is then considered "paid-up" and no future deposits are required. Typically, this type of consumer may be thinking self-insurance is the best option vs. gambling that many years of insurance premiums may not pay off if care is never needed.

If this is the way you are feeling, you'll be glad to know this "almost too good to be true" type of funding method is actually available in a specially designed life insurance policy to help pay for long-term care expenses. Here's how it works:

Issue ages for single individuals generally begin about 30, and joint policies for two people (e.g., mother and daughter, as well as spouses) can be written, if the average age of the two people falls within certain parameters. Age 80 is typically the maximum issue age, although there is no age limit for the benefit payments once a policy is issued. Money can be used to make the single premium deposit with cash, CDs, money market accounts, nonqualified and qualified annuities, or IRAs and Keogh plans. You may also be able to move the cash value from another life insurance policy into this one with no adverse tax consequences. Issue ages can vary based on the source of the premium (i.e., older issue ages of 59 ½ may be required for transfers from qualified annuities, IRAs and Keoghs).

The idea of this policy is that whatever amount you deposit purchases a death benefit like any other life insurance policy. What's new and different is that at least double the amount of your deposit becomes immediately available to you for long-term care. If you need the benefit for long-term care almost immediately, the policy could pay as much as four years of benefits for you at 2% per month of the long-term care amount. The longer you have the policy without filing a claim, the more accumulation and the longer your benefit period. While minimum deposits can be in the $10,000–$20,000 range, a meaningful benefit based on today's costs requires somewhere in the $100,000 range for a 60-year-old couple. A $100,000 deposit provides a monthly benefit for about four years of approximately $5,000 each, a meaningful amount if both spouses need long-term care. Smaller deposits, such as $50,000 or less, can be made if you are willing to self-insure a significant part of your long-term care expense. For added flexibility there usually is a certain amount of money available each year that can be accessed without surrender penalties. (Surrender penalties are graded downward each year until they disappear after 10 years or so.) Withdrawals from gain are subject to income tax. If you elect not to take withdrawals, the money will grow tax deferred, which means it will grow faster than in savings accounts, CDs, money market funds, or similar taxable accounts. This growth is designed to help with inflation.

The pitfalls? If care is needed in the early years of the policy, the insured can expect a benefit period of about four years, instead of longer benefit periods, such as lifetime, which means unlimited. However, newer versions of this policy provide an option to allow the policy to pay benefits for an unlimited number of years if you pay the extra premium for that option, or intervals in between such as five, seven, eight or ten years.

Other pitfalls? Inflation coverage can be tricky. One company allows you to buy a rider that enables you to purchase a 5% increase in the prior year's amount each year without checking your health. The offer stops when it's declined once, and you will be continually putting money into the policy each year that you do accept it. Another company allows you to purchase a rider that extends your benefit period to either eight years or unlimited by creating an additional monthly benefit that won't be available until the base plan is used up. This extension of benefits rider also includes an inflation rider that *increases only that additional monthly benefit 5% compounded, not the base plan.* The reasoning is that the base plan grows through the dividends. Thanks to this new option, you now get inflation protection two different ways with this type of policy, a feature that many people think is essential because of the rapid growth of home health and nursing home costs.

Premium for these optional riders may be included in the lump-sum deposit, or paid separately and ongoing even if you made a lump-sum deposit, depending on the insurance company offering the product. If the premium for the rider is ongoing, the good news is that the premium is guaranteed not to ever go up, so it is a budgetable expense.

Effect of the 1996 Health Insurance Portability and Accountability Act (HIPAA)

This recent legislation allows benefit payments to be totally tax-free as long as benefits do not exceed the greater of $200 per day in 2001 or actual costs. The separate premium for options as described above that extend the benefit period and/or increase the inflation coverage may be taken from the cash value of the policy and if it is, a portion may be taxable income to you. (If you are under age 59½, that amount is normally also subject to a 10% federal surtax.) This premium for the options is the only part of the premium that will be treated as a medical expense and eligible for a tax deduction if medical expenses exceed 7.5% of your adjusted gross income.

With the main portion of the policy, however, you get the best of both worlds—tax-deferred growth and tax-free benefits—which many people think far outweighs having just the premium for the extra inflation/benefit period extension rider as a potential tax deduction or as taxable income. People who are thinking about self-insuring especially like this policy because if long-term care is never needed, the money goes tax-free to your beneficiary as it is paid out in the form of a death benefit. Or, if for any reason you decide to cancel the policy, the guaranteed surrender value is never less than the single premium you paid, less any long-term care benefit payments, of course. If you need long-term care, however, there is a multiplier that makes the money available to pay long-term care benefits worth much more than the face value of the policy.

If you don't want to make a lump-sum payment, newer versions of this product are available with annual and 10-pay premiums as well.

Long-Term Care Insurance and Estate Planning

One company that sells this type of policy has a suggestion to help you with estate planning: Make your adult child owner and beneficiary of a 10-pay policy with you as the insured. Give the child the premium each year through the $10,000 annual gift tax exclusion. Your accomplishments are four-fold:

▲ You accomplish the $10,000 annual gift to decrease the size of your taxable estate.

▲ The policy is not includable in your estate because you are neither the owner nor the beneficiary.

▲ Your long-term care needs are taken care of if you fund the policy adequately:

▲ Your child will receive a significant death benefit if you never need long-term care.

Moreover, many estate planners recommend aggressive gifting, but many people are just not comfortable with gifting assets without a source to pay long-term care costs. Therefore, long-term care insurance, particularly the "nothing to lose, everything to gain" policy described in this section, may play a vital role in constructing and preserving a carefully crafted estate plan that requires aggressive gifting.

For example, those of you who have large estate tax problems could make the benefits of this policy payable to an irrevocable trust with your children as beneficiary, and just pay the long-term care costs yourself, which will further reduce your taxable estate. However, the benefits of the policy going into the irrevocable trust execute a large, tax-free gift to your children.

A June 1997 article in an estate planning magazine summarized the advantages of the single-premium life insurance policy, which the authors referred to as "deposit-based long-term care insurance."[6] The article said by moving emergency funds that would otherwise be invaded for a long-term care need into a deposit-based long-term care policy, you would:

1) preserve your principal;
2) have immediate access to the funds;
3) earn a modest return;
4) create a death benefit; and
5) most importantly, in the event of a long-term care need, multiply the value of these emergency funds by 200+ percent, depending on your age when you are issued a policy.

Your tax advisor can tell you if any of these ideas are helpful for your situation.

Long-Term Care Annuities

A long-term care **deferred** annuity can play a huge role in helping people who cannot qualify for long-term care insurance due to age or health problems. This annuity is available to age 85 and there are seven, very broad health questions that will not be difficult for most people to satisfy. The questions deal with major conditions like dementia, Parkinson's disease, multiple sclerosis, Lou Gehrig's disease, and whether or not you are dependent on a walker or wheelchair or are bedridden. Being in a nursing home in the past two years would disqualify you, but having a couple of weeks of home health care in that same time frame would not.

This concept uses an annuity with two funds. One fund, which is for long-term care expenses, grows at a high interest rate, 9% as of January, 2000, with a five-year rate guarantee, then current interest thereafter. (A 9% rate is equal to 12.86% in a taxable fund for someone in a combined 30% tax bracket.) The other fund, which is just the regular cash fund in an annuity, grows at the guaranteed rate of 3%. The five-year jumpstart on the long-term care fund ensures a higher amount available for long-term care. At the end of the fifth year, you decide if you want the strategy of growing the LTC fund at a higher rate to continue, or if you want to equalize the growth rate between the two funds. (The funds are automatically equalized around your 90th birthday.)

The purpose of the separate LTC fund is to allow you immediate access to the money for services from a licensed home health care agency, adult day care center, assisted living facility or nursing home care. Otherwise, early withdrawals from an annuity mean limitations on the amount you can withdraw, usually 10%, without penalty.

Benefits begin after only a 7-day waiting period when your doctor verifies that you either need help with at least two of six Activities of Daily Living (bathing, continence, dressing, eating, toileting and transferring) or you are cognitively impaired. The benefit is reimbursement, not indemnity, which means it will pay no more than actual expenses up to the monthly limit for a minimum of 36 months (18 months if a joint policy and both annuitants are receiving care at the same time). There is a lifetime rider available if you are willing to pay the additional premium.

Here's an example of how LTC withdrawals will be calculated:

$100,000   (LTC fund balance at time of claim)

÷   34.5   (factor to ensure a minimum of 36 months of coverage)

$2,898   per month available benefit for actual expenses

Money withdrawn from the LTC fund reduces the cash fund proportionally. For example, a $3,000 withdrawal from the LTC fund means a $1,500 withdrawal from the cash fund. Conversely, a $1,500 withdrawal from the cash fund means a $3,000 withdrawal from the LTC fund.

If you do not use up all of the money on long-term care, the amount remaining in the cash fund will be passed to your beneficiary outside of probate at your death, or the surviving annuitant (second-to-die) if it is a joint contract.

This product is a deferred annuity, which many people prefer over low-interest bearing accounts like CDs and money market funds because of the tax-deferred earnings. Having this product in place with money that you keep for an emergency anyway could give you the flexibility to have a longer waiting period on a traditional LTC policy. Some companies offer longer waiting periods in those states that allow it of 180 days, 365 days or even 730 days.

Since it is a deferred annuity, you are taxed on the gain as withdrawals are made.

Now for a pitfall. This product was introduced as a non-tax-qualified long-term care policy. That means you are at risk of being taxed on the money that is dispersed from the LTC fund if the IRS rules against non-qualified policies. Beware of anyone telling you that you can deduct all of your LTC expenses as medical expenses at tax time so it really doesn't matter. **This is a reimbursement policy,** which means it will only make a payment from the LTC fund when a claim for an actual service or charge is presented, so it is directly reimbursing long-term care expenses. There's a very good chance the IRS would disqualify your deduction for medical expenses, because IRS Form 1040, Schedule A—Itemized Deductions plainly says *"Caution: Do not include expenses reimbursed or paid by others."*

This book in no way intends to give tax advice, so please see your personal tax advisor for an opinion on how this policy would apply to you.

If the product were changed to satisfy the benefit criteria of a tax-qualified policy (i.e., mainly that benefits are available when your doctor or a registered nurse or licensed social worker certifies that you are expected to be unable to perform at least two Activities of Daily Living for at least 90 days, or that you have a severe cognitive impairment), this product could present a very interesting option for long-term care financing, especially for people with significant health problems. It also has added flexibility in that the 10% allowable annual withdrawals from the cash fund give you money to use for associated costs with long-term care that are not covered as an eligible long-term care expense, such as prescription drugs and miscellaneous supplies.

Other advantages over other annuities that allow withdrawals for long-term care expenses are that they may allow withdrawals only for nursing home expenses after an extended stay such as six months, and the LTC fund may not have as high a growth rate as in this new LTC annuity. If you consider switching from another annuity to this one, exchanges are possible from single annuitant to single annuitant but not from single annuitant to the joint policy.

A final caution on this product, as with all the life insurance products discussed in this section, is to make sure you put enough money into it to accommodate inflation needs. Project the average cost for care in your area at a 5.8% compounded annual growth rate for the time frame in which you think you may need to access the LTC fund, which will be largely determined by your age (10, 15, 20 years, etc.).

A long-term care **immediate** annuity is available even to people already receiving long-term care, for example, a nursing home patient. This concept involves making a single premium which is converted into a monthly income guaranteed for the life of the policyholder. You can even select an annual rate for the payment to increase anywhere from 1%–10% to provide for inflation.

Why would anyone want to do this and what makes this type of annuity different than a regular immediate annuity? Here's the main reason: A regular annuity is not medically underwritten and the same life expectancy tables are applied to everyone, regardless of medical condition. So an 80-year-old female desiring a monthly benefit of $3,000 would normally have to pay almost $300,000 in a single premium.   However, if she had severe Alzheimer's, this special long-term care annuity would require only $97,000 to obtain the same $3,000 monthly benefit. You can even structure the annuity so that your beneficiary will receive a portion of the money if you die earlier than the insurance company thought you would. Of course, you should seek advice from a professional tax advisor about the tax consequences before pursuing an option of this nature.

Variable Annuity/LTC Policies

Still looking for a policy that answers the "use it or lose it" objection in your mind, but haven't found one that exactly meets your needs? Several "variable" deferred long-term care annuities are available, and "variable" means that you get to select how you want the money you deposit into your annuity invested. Choices typically revolve around a collection of mutual funds and just like any other investment vehicle, the performance of these funds influence the benefit payout.

Regardless of how these alternative funding mechanisms for long-term care are set up, tying the long-term care benefits to life insurance or annuities with a single fund makes inflation coverage tricky and can disappoint as utilization of long-term care benefits reduces the death benefit or the annuity balance. The newest innovation is to offer long-term care insurance with a variable annuity, yet keep the accounts separate so that utilization of either side doesn't reduce the other side; i.e., annuity withdrawals don't lower the long-term care benefit and a long-term care claim doesn't drain the annuity side. For example, a 55-year-old might purchase a variable long-term care annuity of this type with a premium of $58,900. Of this premium, $33,671 would go to the long-term care insurance side and $25,229 would go to the variable annuity. At age 85, she would have about $166,313, assuming an 8% gross investment return before taxes in the annuity side of her policy, if she had made no withdrawals to that point. She could then withdraw $100,000 to take her grandchildren on a trip, then have a stroke the week they get back and she would still have her full benefits for long-term care available, even though she had just taken $100,000 out of the annuity side. If death occurs in the early years of the policy, a death benefit kicks in to supplement the annuity balance in order to return the original investment to her estate.

The Health Insurance Portability and Accountability Act of 1996 prohibits a long-term care insurance policy from providing for a cash surrender value, so the IRS is considering the tax qualification status. Since it involves two completely separate accounts, one for the annuity side and one for the long-term care insurance benefits, and the use of either side does not affect the balance of the other side, there may be a positive outcome to the question.

This long-term care insurance/variable annuity combo is intended for clients with incomes above $75,000 and assets above $300,000, and particularly for clients who are familiar with investment strategies who find the choice of 40 major funds attractive for the annuity portion.

Reverse Mortgages

Since the majority of older Americans own their homes and have paid off their mortgages, many people find themselves "cash poor" and "house rich." Because of these characteristics, a certain amount of activity is occurring in the marketplace to help people tap the value of the home without giving it up as long as they live in it. Converting the equity of the home into cash can be accomplished either through sale plans or loan plans. The sale plans, which involve selling the home then leasing it back as long as the seller is able to live in it, are not popular for tax reasons. It's possible that the IRS will not view the plan as a bona fide sale if the house is not sold at fair market price, or if the buyer is receiving favorable treatment, or if the buyer does not assume full ownership until the death of the seller. If the IRS does not view the plan as a bona fide sale, the one-time capital gains exclusion is not available to the seller. In other words, people sometimes try to give their kids a bargain, and the IRS doesn't look favorably at special deals for children or any other buyers.

Home equity conversion loans in the form of reverse mortgages are available, in which no repayment of the loan is generally required until the borrower dies, sells the home, or permanently moves. Started by the federal government in 1988 to help older Americans on fixed incomes, the program allows homeowners over 62 to "cash in" on their home equity. You must be a single-family homeowner, which can include a condominium or town-house as long as the development meets FHA guidelines. Others who are not on a fixed income also see the benefits of "cashing in" on the equity in their home for additional investments. There are no income qualifications and limited credit qualifications, because unlike an equity loan from a bank, a reverse mortgage requires no monthly payments.

The monies available to the homeowner are tax free and don't count as income for Social Security eligibility purposes. The balance due grows as monies are disbursed to the homeowner. The funds can be disbursed in several ways. Cash available can be taken in monthly payments over a period of years, a lifetime, or as a line of credit you can draw down as needed over a number of years. You can even receive a combination of regular monthly payments and a line of credit. You still own the home. It can be sold at any time (for example, if you decide to move) and when sold, any balance due on the reverse mortgage is paid and the remaining equity goes to you or in the case of your death, to your estate. Equity remaining would depend on how long you remain in the home and the value of the home at the time of sale.

The reverse mortgage market is poised to grow substantially as the baby boomers move into their retirement years. As of this writing, there are four products available but that will increase to meet various demands of clients. Presently the most widely used product is FHA's Home Equity Conversion Mortgage (HECM). The Federal National Mortgage Association, known as "FannieMae," offers a product called the Home Keeper. FannieMae doesn't make direct loans. It buys loans from lenders, packages them and resells them to investors. Financial Freedom, headquartered in Irvine, California, offers two private reverse mortgage products.

According to a November 9, 1995, article in *USA Today*, "The older you are and the more valuable your home, the more you can borrow." Each program has a "lending limit" and the amount available to the client depends on age, and in some programs, on the number of borrowers (but all have to be over 62). It also depends on the value of the home and the interest rate used to calculate that amount. For example, in the FHA program, a 74-year-old in a $180,000 home could gain access to $98,820, which could be set up as monthly income or as a line of credit. FannieMae offers two options—that same borrower could get $77,760 in the equity share program and $61,576 in the non-equity share. The "equity share" provides more money on the front end, but there is a penalty on the back end. The "non-equity share" provides less money on the front end and no penalty payment on the back end. FannieMae is utilized more frequently by older, single people than by married people. The Financial Freedom products are geared to higher valued homes, so borrowers who are 74 and 76 who live in a $500,000 home for example, could be approved for $127,326 to $133,548.

If you take the money in monthly payments but live so long that the payments exceed the home's value, you or your heirs do not have to pay back any amount larger than the worth of your home. After you die, your children (or other heirs) can keep the home if they like—they just have to pay the balance in full. They can pay off the reverse mortgage using their own money or they can sell your house. If they sell your house for more than is owed, they can keep the difference.

The interest rates on reverse mortgages are adjustable. Interest adds to the balance that will be owed when the property is sold. FHA offers either an annual or monthly adjustable interest rate and FannieMae has only a monthly adjustable. FHA's rate is the weekly average of the one-year Treasury Bill plus a margin of 1.2% for the monthly adjustable or 2.1% for the annual. For example, on April 24, 2000, the one-year T-Bill was 6.14%, so the annual rate was 8.24%. (Since 1985, the highest FHA monthly adjustable rate has been 9.26% and the lowest was 4.62%.) FannieMae's rate is the weekly average of the one-month CD rate plus a margin of 3.40%. The one-month CD rate on April 24th was 6.07%, so the rate for a FannieMae reverse mortgage was 9.5%. Monthly adjustments to this interest rate will not affect monthly payments (but this may effect credit lines, if you choose to take your money as a line of credit). This will only effect how much money is owed when you die or move out of your home.

A list of lenders and an informational brochure is available by calling FannieMae at 1-800-732-6643.

To make sure families understand the program, FHA requires a free individual information meeting with a HUD-approved housing agency separate from the lender so you can learn about the program objectively and decide if it's right for you. Paulette Wisch at Financial Freedom (303-843-0480 or 800-843-0480) can give you a free no-obligation package of information with a list of the HUD agencies.

Most of the cash from the various plans has been used for home repairs, to weatherize homes, to make homes accessible for the handicapped, for basic living expenses, and some of the money is being used to fund long-term care services. Rather than pay for the long-term care services directly, much more "mileage" can be obtained from the money by purchasing long-term care insurance if you are insurable. You can purchase a long-term care policy outright by paying a monthly, semi-annual or annual premium, or a lump-sum obtained from a reverse mortgage can be used to purchase an annuity, which can then be set up to pay the LTC premiums for the rest of the insured's life. Or, the lump sum can be used to purchase a life insurance or annuity long-term care policy as described on pp. 162-174 that pays LTC expenses with a guaranteed premium.

Your State Agency on Aging also has information on organizations to contact if you are interested in obtaining a reverse mortgage. The June 1997 AARP bulletin contained a warning from Andrew Cuomo, the Department of Housing and Urban Development (HUD) secretary. Mr. Cuomo cautions against salespeople contacting you to do a reverse mortgage and charging hefty fees for information and forms that HUD offers free. He said the legal limit for counseling and referral services is $50, and you should not be charged more than that. If you suspect a scam, you can check out the organization that contacted you by calling HUD directly toll-free at 1-888-466-3487, and HUD will investigate at no charge to you.

In summary, one funding method for long-term care does not fit all. Since this is America, it's safe to say that we will continue to see much product innovation and variety throughout this century as our country struggles to find a way to pay for long-term care with private funding as much as possible and prevent unprecedented taxation—the inevitable result if the baby boomers wind up on any kind of public assistance for long-term care.

People Who Do Not Qualify for LTC Insurance

People with significant health issues may not be able to qualify for a long-term care policy. Here are some suggestions:

▲ Apply with another insurance company. Seek a company that doesn't just say "yes" or "no." There are companies that will sell you a policy for extra premium or will issue you a policy with an alternative benefit offer—perhaps a three-year or five-year benefit period instead of lifetime, or a 100-day waiting period instead of 20 or 60 days.

The majority of long-term care claims are less than three years so a policy with a shorter benefit period may work out fine for you. However long your policy will pay is that much time for you to be a private-pay patient, which will increase your choices and independence.

▲ The new long-term care annuities discussed in this section may be an especially good option for you since some of them use very light underwriting and one will provide benefits even if you already need long-term care.

▲ A viatical or life settlement as discussed in this section may be an option for you if you have any type of life insurance.

▲   A reverse mortgage as discussed in this section may be an option if you have your home paid off or almost paid off.

▲   There are annuities on the market that have no surrender charges if the withdrawal is used for nursing home expenses.

▲   Seek the advice of a good elder-law attorney and your State Agency on Aging. Contact the National Academy of Elder Law Attorneys, 1604 North Country Club Road, Tucson, Arizona 85716 or go to www.naela.org for a national registry of elder-law attorneys.

Where Do I Go from Here?

To choose the best long-term care insurance policy, call an insurance agent you can trust. Call as soon as you can to take advantage of rates based on your current age and your good health. Health is our most precious asset. Once health problems occur, it can be impossible to get a good insurance policy, especially a long-term care policy.

Martin K. Bayne is a former insurance agent who was stricken with Parkinson's disease in his forties. He has used this unkind affliction to help millions from his home by spending sometimes 20 hours a day building the most comprehensive web site for long-term care issues in the world. He is more commonly known as Mr. Long-Term Care at www.mrltc.com., and works diligently to raise the awareness of how essential it is to plan ahead for long-term care. After living with Parkinson's disease for five years, his is a voice in the wilderness that is being heard around the world:

For decades, most of us have lived in denial regarding the physical, emotional and financial trauma, that often characterizes LTC. We refuse to talk openly about the possibility of someday needing protracted medical care. Instead, we say, I'll never have a stroke or develop Alzheimer's disease. Even if I do, the Veteran's Administration or Medicare or my Elk's Lodge or children will take care of me. After all, we reason, I'm sure that after working and paying taxes for 40 years, I'm at least entitled to some kind of care.

Tragically, the ultimate consequence of that denial is often both traumatic and unnecessary to the individual, their spouse and family, and their community.*

So, go to the telephone and call for help today. Do it now, for yourself, but mostly for your family.

* "Jousting with Dragons: A Manifesto" by Martin K. Bayne

Appendix A:
Senior Benefits

Medicare Benefits

~~~~~~

Medicare, a federal program, is the cornerstone of the older American's health care benefits and is available to all Americans at age 65. Some people think Medicare is sufficient to handle their health care financing needs, but as this chapter will show the program has some very big gaps—gaps that can leave you with huge bills if you are not prepared. The largest gap is long-term care, according to LifePlans, Inc., one of the nation's leading research firms for long-term care issues.[1]

Enrolling for Medicare

Most Americans are automatically enrolled for Medicare when they reach age 65. Your Medicare card shows you the effective date of your coverage. The program is administered by the Health Care Financing Administration (HCFA) of the U.S. Department of Health and Human Services. The Social Security Administration provides information about the program and handles enrollment. You should contact your local Social Security office for information at least three months before you turn 65. You can also call the Social Security toll-free number 1-800-772-1213 any business day from 7 a.m. to 7 p.m. EST if you have questions about Medicare eligibility or need enrollment information.

Two Parts of Medicare

Medicare has two separate parts. **Part A** covers inpatient-type care—inpatient hospitalization, skilled nursing facility stays, psychiatric hospitalization, as well as hospice care and home health care. **Part B** covers medical services—physician services, related medical services and supplies, outpatient hospital treatment, X-rays and laboratory tests, ambulance services, physical, occupational and speech therapy, mental health services and Pap smears.

Part A is financed through part of the Social Security (FICA) tax paid by all workers and their employers. You do not have to pay a monthly premium for Medicare Part A if you or your spouse are entitled to benefits under either the Social Security or Railroad Retirement systems, or have worked a sufficient period of time in federal, state or local government employment to be insured. If you do not meet the qualifications for premium-free Part A benefits, you may purchase the coverage if you are at least age 65 and meet certain requirements. The Part A premium for 2001 is $300 per month if you have less than 29 quarters of Social Security coverage. It is $165 per month for 30–39 quarters.

Part B is optional and is offered to all beneficiaries when they become entitled to premium-free Part A. It may also be purchased by most people age 65 or over who do not qualify for premium-free Part A coverage. (Note: If you purchase Part A, you must purchase Part B as well.) The Part B premium in 2001 is $50 each month and is deducted from your Social Security or Railroad Retirement check.

You are automatically enrolled in Part B when you become entitled to Part A unless you state that you don't want it. Although you do not have to purchase Part B, it is an excellent buy because the federal government pays 75% of the program costs.[2] Your Medicare card will show the coverage you have—Hospital Insurance (Part A), Medical Insurance (Part B) or both—and the date your coverage started. If you have only one part of Medicare, you can get information about getting the other part from your local Social Security office.

If you are still covered under an employer's health insurance plan after you are 65 or because you or your spouse is still working, you should accept Part A Medicare but elect to postpone enrolling for Part B until you are no longer covered through the group. You will save the Part B premium of $50 a month. Once you retire or your group insurance terminates (whichever comes first), you have eight months to enroll in Part B without a penalty. Contact your Social Security office as soon as you know your group coverage is going to end to obtain the necessary forms: 1) for the employer to certify that you have had group coverage and 2) for you to complete indicating that you now want Part B. If you are not covered by an employer's health plan, you should enroll in Part B during your initial enrollment period, which is the seven-month period beginning three months before you are first able to get Medicare. For most people, this means three months before the 65th birthday. If you don't accept Part B during that seven month period, you will have to wait until the next general enrollment period to enroll (January 1 through March 31 of each year). Your premium will be 10% higher for each year you wait, and the coverage won't begin until the following July. For more detailed information about how Medicare works with other benefits such as group plans, VA benefits, TRICARE (formerly CHAMPUS), or any other plan, ask your Social Security office for a copy of *Medicare and Other Health Benefits: Who Pays First?* This booklet is published by the Health Care Financing Administration, U.S. Department of Health and Human Services.

Individuals younger than 65 can get Medicare solely on the basis of permanent kidney failure or after two years of receiving Social Security Disability benefits. To get a free copy of *Medicare Coverage of Kidney Dialysis and Kidney Transplant Services*, write to Medicare Publications, Health Care Financing Administration, 7500 Security Blvd., Baltimore, MD 21244-1850, or visit the official Medicare website at www.medicare.gov. If you have questions about specific Medicare requirements or benefit features, be sure to consult *Medicare and You*, which is available from any Social Security Administration office, by calling 1-800-MEDICARE (800-633-4227) or by writing to Medicare Publications at the address above you can also visit the official Medicare website at www.medicare.gov.

The Medicare Gaps

When Medicare was created, Congress determined that the patient should share in paying for the cost of the care he or she received. The underlying concept is simple: If the patient shares in the costs of care, he or she will be more likely to use the benefits wisely. So, the program was designed with deductible and coinsurance amounts the patient must pay.

In the first years of the Medicare program, these deductible and coinsurance charges were moderate amounts. But after more than three decades of annual increases, these charges can add up to a major expense. For example:

▲ You must pay the first $792 of your bill when you are hospitalized.

▲ You must pay $99 each day for days 21 through 100 in a skilled nursing facility.

▲ You must pay the first $100 of the Medicare-approved amounts for doctor services, medical supplies and equipment, outpatient services and ambulance.

▲ You must pay 20% of the cost of your bills for doctor services, medical supplies and equipment, outpatient services and ambulance.

▲ You must pay charges above the Medicare-approved amount billed by doctors who do not accept Medicare assignment (up to a 115% cap—see p. 191).

▲ In addition to your 20% co-payment, you must pay all costs for physical or occupational therapy provided by independent therapists (outside a nursing home or hospital) in excess of Medicare's maximum annual allowance. The annual allowance is limited to $1,500 through 2002, and physical therapy would include speech therapy.

These expenses can add up quickly, and this is only a representative sample of some of the most common Medicare gaps. In addition to financial gaps caused by the deductible and coinsurance amounts, there are also gaps caused by coverage limitations and administrative considerations.

Medicare-Approved Charges

One of the most misunderstood aspects of Medicare is the way doctor charges are determined.

All of your doctor's charges may not be considered eligible for the 80% Medicare Part B reimbursement. Medicare payment is based on the Medicare-approved amounts, not the actual charges billed by the physician or medical supplier. The Medicare-approved amount is based on a national fee schedule. This schedule assigns a value to each physician service based on the specific service performed, his or her medical practice costs, malpractice insurance costs and a geographical factor. Each time you go to the physician, the amount Medicare will recognize for that service will be taken from the national fee schedule. Medicare will generally pay 80% of that amount. (Example: The doctor charges $100. Medicare may approve $70 and pay 80%, which means that Medicare would actually pay $56.)

Doctors who take assignment on a Medicare claim agree to accept the Medicare-approved amount as payment in full. They are paid directly by Medicare, and you pay them any deductible or coinsurance amount due. Ask your doctor if he or she accepts Medicare assignment.

Many physicians and suppliers accept assignment on a case-by-case basis. If your physician or supplier does not accept assignment, you are responsible for the bill, and Medicare will reimburse you. However, physicians who do not accept assignment of a Medicare claim are reimbursed at a lower level and are limited by law as to the amount they can charge you for covered services. The most a non-participating physician can charge you for services covered by Medicare is 115% of the fee schedule amount. (Some states also have special laws that limit how much physicians can charge—Connecticut, Massachusetts, Minnesota, New York, Ohio, Pennsylvania, Rhode Island and Vermont. Check with your state's insurance department or office on aging for more information. See **Who to Call for Help**, p. 225.)

Regardless of whether physicians accept assignment, they are required to file your Medicare claims for you. If they accept assignment, Medicare pays the physician and sends you a notice, called an Explanation of Medicare Benefits (EOMB), to let you know how much was paid. If the doctor does not accept assignment, Medicare pays you and you pay the doctor the amount Medicare paid plus all permissible charges, which may include your $100 calendar year deductible for Part B, your 20% co-payment, and any charge above the Medicare-approved amount up to the 115% cap. Only Medicare-approved amounts count toward the $100 Part B deductible, not the actual charges billed by the physician or medical supplier.

You may contact the insurance company that administers the Medicare Part B program in your area for a list of the doctors in your area who take assignment. However, it's still a good idea to check with the doctor when you make an appointment because the doctor may have stopped taking assignment since the list was printed.

After January 1, 1998, patients may enter into private contracts with doctors who do not participate in Medicare at least two years after the private contract is signed as long as the claim is not filed with Medicare or with Medicare supplemental insurance. **In this situation, you agree to be responsible for all charges and no limits apply to the amount you can be charged by the doctor for his or her services.**

Be Informed

As shown above, Medicare does not pay the entire cost for all services covered by the program. You or your Medicare supplemental insurance must pay certain deductible and coinsurance amounts and charges in excess of Medicare's approved amount. When you are enrolled in Medicare and Medicare supplement insurance, you will receive complete details on the limitations and exclusions of Medicare. Be sure to read that information carefully. As with any insurance plan, understanding your benefit provisions up front helps you avoid many financial and administrative problems when you file claims. **So, carefully read your Medicare and Medicare Supplemental insurance literature.**

Appeals

If you don't agree with how Medicare handles a claim or if you think more should have been paid, you have the right to appeal the claim. Best results are obtained if you send a letter from your doctor with your appeal. Just ask the doctor to write a letter that further justifies the services performed. Many times an appeal results in an additional payment. Send the appeal to the Medicare carrier listed on your Medicare Explanation of Medical Benefits.

2001 Medicare Benefits

Medicare Part A

HEALTH CARE FACILITY SERVICES

Medicare pays:

Inpatient Hospital Services, Semi-Private Room and Board, Miscellaneous Hospital Services and Supplies, Drugs, X-Rays, Lab Tests

All but $792 during 1st 60 days of a benefit period.*

All but $198 a day for 61st through 90th day of a benefit period.*

All but $396 a day for 91st through 150th day of a benefit period* (while using the 60-day Medicare lifetime reserve)

Post Hospital **Skilled Nursing Facility Care** for a Medicare Approved Stay in a Medicare Approved Facility

All costs for first 20 days of a benefit period.*

All but $99 a day for 21st through 100th day of a benefit period.*

*BENEFIT PERIOD: A new benefit period begins after you have been out of a hospital or skilled nursing facility for 60 days in a row.

Blood

All but first three pints during a calendar year.

Home Health Care

Pays only for visits that begin within 14 days after discharge from a hospital or skilled nursing facility, limited to 100 visits

194

per episode of care. (A new episode of care won't begin until the patient has received no hospital, skilled nursing facility, or home health services for 60 consecutive days.) Visits are paid for a nurse or home health aide as long as skilled care is needed at least once every 60 days. (Drawing blood is no longer considered a skilled service.) Also pays for part-time services for physical therapy, speech therapy, nutritional counseling, respiratory therapy. (Note: The Balanced Budget Act of 1997 establishes guidelines for frequency and duration of home health visits. <u>Visits will be denied that exceed the standard.</u>) Patient must be homebound. Medical equipment paid at 80%.

Hospice
(Available to patients certified terminally ill.)

Unlimited benefits. No deductible for physician services, nursing care, medical appliances and supplies, counseling, and home health aide and homemaker services. Pays all but 5% of cost of outpatient drugs or $5 per prescription, whichever is lower. (Inpatient respite care is limited to five days per stay, and hospice does not pay for ongoing eight-hour shifts of non-skilled home care.)

Medicare Part B

PHYSICIANS' CHARGES:	**Medicare pays:**
Services of a **Physician, Nurse Practitioner and Physician Assistant**	80% of reasonable charges after $100 annual deductible, except 50% for mental health visits.
Outpatient Services and Medical Supplies (Other Than Blood and Immunosuppressive Therapy Drugs), Ambulance	Reasonable charges are determined by Medicare. Sometimes they are called Medicare-approved charges or Medicare-eligible expenses.
Blood	80% of Medicare-approved amount after $100 deductible after 1st three pints.
Home Health Care	Covers home health care if the patient does not have Part A. Otherwise, only visits beyond the first 100 visits or visits that do not follow a hospital or skilled nursing facility stay paid at 100%. These services are still subject to guidelines for frequency and duration.
Preventive Services	Covers annual mammograms after age 40 and pap smears and pelvic exams at least every three years. Covers colorectal cancer screening and blood glucose testing strips. Covers diabetes self-management tests and bone mass measurements for certain conditions. Prostate cancer screening covered 1/1/2000.

Co-payment and Part B
deductible apply, except no
deductible for mammograms,
pap smears or pelvic exams.

MISCELLANEOUS: **Medicare Pays:**

Immunosuppressive Drugs   80% of reasonable charges after
(Drugs after Organ Transplant) $100 deductible.
and Some Oral Cancer Drugs

Medicare pays only for services it determines to be medically necessary and only the amount it determines to be reasonable.

Reimbursement to hospitals is based on a pre-established amount based on the diagnosis of the patient's condition, which is called a prospective payment system. If you are discharged earlier than expected, the hospital makes money. If you stay longer than the standard, the hospital loses money. For this reason, doctors are under tremendous pressure to get the patient out of the hospital as soon as possible. The Balanced Budget Act of 1997 also requires nursing homes and home health agencies to be paid under a prospective payment system, beginning 10/1/00 for home health agencies and phased in for nursing homes between 7/1/98 and 2002.

Reimbursement to physicians is based on a national fee schedule that began 1/1/99 and will be fully implemented by 2002. Doctors who "accept assignment" do not bill patients for amounts above the fee schedule. After 1/1/98, patients may enter into private contracts with doctors who do not participate in Medicare at least two years after the contract as long as the claim is not filed with Medicare or with Medicare supplemental insurance.

Expenses Not Covered By Medicare

Medicare does not provide benefits for:

▲   private duty nursing at home or in the hospital

▲   skilled nursing home costs beyond 100 days unless you stop receiving skilled care 60 days in a row

▲   custodial or intermediate nursing home costs (non-skilled care)

▲   physician charges above Medicare's approved amount

▲   most outpatient drugs*

▲   care received outside the U.S., except under certain conditions in Canada and Mexico

▲   dental care or dentures, checkups except preventive services as named on the preceding page, most routine immunizations (except flu shots, pneumonia vaccines and hepatitus part B are covered), homemaker services, cosmetic surgery, routine foot care, examinations for and the cost of eyeglasses or hearing aids

* There are three main sources for outpatient drug coverage through private insurance. At least fifty percent of Medicare beneficiaries had some level of drug benefits in 1995, either through retiree health plans, the high option "H, I and J" Medicare supplement plans, or through a health maintenance organization (HMO).[3] The following sections provide additional information about these options.

Medicare Supplement Policies

M edicare supplement policies, sometimes referred to as "Medigap" coverage, are individual policies from private insurance companies that are designed to pay the coinsurance amounts, deductibles and other gaps **after Medicare benefits have been provided.** And that's the caution—Medicare supplements are designed to pay only after Medicare has made a payment. With a few exceptions, they typically do not pay for services not covered by Medicare. Medicare supplemental insurance policies can be valuable, however, as Medicare alone will not pay most of a patient's medical expenses.

Do You Need a Medicare Supplement?

Medicare supplements are purchased by more than a third of Medicare beneficiaries to fill gaps in benefits under the traditional Medicare program,[4] but there are four types of people who do not need a Medicare supplement:

▲ *Low-income individuals* can get the Medicare Part A and Part B deductibles and coinsurance payments and the Part B premium paid by their state Medicaid program. "Low-income" means your annual income is below the national poverty level and your assets (not counting your home) are less than $4,000 ($6,000 for couples).

The 2000 federal income guidelines for this program are $716 a month for individuals, and $958 a month for couples. These amounts are higher for Alaska ($890 individual/$1,192 couple) and Hawaii ($820 individual/$1,098 couple). You can call 1-800-MEDICARE (800-633-4227) for 2001 income requirements. Note: All of these amounts include an additional $20, which is called "a monthly Supplemental Security Income disregard," which just means these are the true amounts of income you can have to qualify for this program.

The exact income amount that qualifies you for this program can vary a little by state, so you should call your local Medicaid office if you think you might qualify, and to obtain current income amounts. If you don't know the telephone number, call your State Agency on Aging and ask for the number to call for information about the Qualified Medicare Beneficiary (QMB) program. (See **Who to Call for Help,** p. 227.)

Note: If your income is too much to qualify for the QMB program, you may still be able to qualify for the Specified Low-Income Medicare Beneficiary (SLMB) program, which will pay your Part B premium of $50 per month in 2001. Your assets still have to be low, but your 2001 income can be as much as $855 for an individual and $1,145 for a couple (Alaska: $1,063 individual/$1,426 couple; Hawaii: $979 individual/$1,313 couple).

▲ *Individuals who are allowed by their employers to continue group health insurance after retiring* usually do not need a separate Medicare supplement policy. Retiree group insurance usually has better benefits (i.e. prescription drugs, hearing aids, vision aids, etc.) than an individual Medicare supplement and the retiree is well covered by the group plan.

▲ *Individuals or spouses who work past age 65* can be covered by an employer's group health plan if the employer has 20+ employees and should elect to do so as group plans are normally better than individual Medicare supplement policies. Upon retirement, the individual can purchase a Medicare supplement policy if the employer does not provide group coverage to retirees.

▲ *Individuals who are enrolled in a Medicare managed care plan* (See **Managed Care Medicare Plans,** p. 215.)

People who either don't meet the low income requirements of the Qualified Medicare Beneficiary program or who are not covered by an employer or former employer or who are not enrolled in a Medicare managed care plan (see p. 213) may consider purchasing a good individual Medicare supplement policy, unless they decide to self-insure balances to Medicare.

Can You Self-Insure Balances to Medicare?

Individuals with significant assets who wish to self-insure balances to Medicare can do so as today balances after Medicare's payment are small. Some people elect to do this because they feel the money they have been using for Medicare supplemental insurance is better spent to pay long-term care insurance premium, because long-term care is a much bigger risk than balances to Medicare.

Disabled Individuals Under Age 65

Disabled individuals under age 65 who qualify for Medicare should contact their state's Department of Insurance for information about Medicare supplement policies. (See *Open Enrollment* on p. 207 for legislation effective 1/1/95 to help disabled people at age 65.)

Federal Guidelines for Medicare Supplements

The insurance industry developed some very fine Medicare supplement policies throughout the history of the Medicare program. But there has also been abuse of this sensitive market. For this reason, older Americans need to be extremely careful when selecting their Medicare supplement insurance policy.

Largely because of these problems, the federal government implemented guidelines in 1992 that require state insurance regulators to require insurance companies operating in their state to simplify the Medicare supplement enrollment process. The federal guidelines say insurance companies can now sell only ten standard policies. (Massachusetts, Minnesota and Wisconsin standardized their Medicare supplement plans earlier and didn't have to conform to the national standardized plans. Residents of these states should contact their state insurance departments to find out their state's version of Medicare supplement coverage.) The ten policies are designated A-J. All insurance companies that sell Medicare supplement insurance have to offer Plan A, also called the "basic policy." The other plans are optional. The basic benefits (Plan A) consist of the following core benefits:

▲ Coverage for the Part A coinsurance amount ($198 per day in 2001) for the 61st through the 90th day of hospitalization in each benefit period.

▲ Coverage for the Part A coinsurance amount ($396 per day in 2001) for each of Medicare's 60 non-renewable lifetime hospital inpatient reserve days used.

▲ After all Medicare hospital benefits are exhausted, coverage for 100% of the Medicare Part A eligible hospital expenses. Coverage is limited to a maximum of 365 days of additional inpatient hospital care during the policyholder's lifetime. The benefit is paid either at the rate Medicare pays hospitals under the Prospective Payment System or another appropriate standard of payment.

▲ Coverage under Medicare Parts A and B for the reasonable cost of the first three pints of blood or equivalent quantities of packed red blood cells per calendar year unless replaced in accordance with federal regulations.

▲ Coverage for the 20% coinsurance amount for Part B services after the $100 annual deductible is met.

The chart on the next page summarizes the standard Medicare supplement plans.

Summary of Standard Medicare Supplement Plans

A	B	C	D	E	F*	G	H	I	J
Basic Benefits	Basic Benefits	Basic Benefits	Basic Benefits	Basic Benefits	Basic Benefits	Basic Benefits	Basic Benefits	Basic Benefits	Basic Benefits
		Skilled Nursing Coinsurance	Skilled Nursing Coinsurance	Skilled Nursing Coinsurance	Skilled Nursing Coinsurance	Skilled Nursing Coinsurance	Skilled Nursing Coinsurance	Skilled Nursing Coinsurance	Skilled Nursing Coinsurance
	Part A Deductible	Part A Deductible	Part A Deductible	Part A Deductible	Part A Deductible	Part A Deductible	Part A Deductible	Part A Deductible	Part A Deductible
		Part B Deductible			Part B Deductible				Part B Deductible
					Part B Excess (100%)	Part B Excess (80%)		Part B Excess (100%)	Part B Excess (100%)
		Foreign Travel Emergency	Foreign Travel Emergency	Foreign Travel Emergency	Foreign Travel Emergency	Foreign Travel Emergency	Foreign Travel Emergency	Foreign Travel Emergency	Foreign Travel Emergency
			At-Home Recovery			At-Home Recovery		At-Home Recovery	At-Home Recovery
							Basic Drugs ($1250 Limit)	Basic Drugs ($1250 Limit)	Extended Drugs ($3000 Limit)
				Preventive Care					Preventive Care

* $1,580 high deductible option for policies issued in 2001.

Features of a Good Medicare Supplement Policy

~~~~~~

With standardized policies, it is much easier to select a good Medicare supplement insurance policy. Nevertheless, the following features are still important considerations when evaluating which Medicare supplement policy you should purchase.

If you already have Medicare and a Medicare supplement policy, this chapter can help you evaluate your current policy. The federal Medicare supplement guidelines only apply to policies sold after their implementation in 1992.

Guaranteed Renewable—This means the policy can never be cancelled as long as you pay the premiums and as long as you answered all the questions in the application truthfully. It can't be cancelled even if you have a lot of claims or even if the insurance company stops selling Medicare supplement insurance. "Conditionally renewable" means your policy can be cancelled under certain conditions, such as if the insurance company cancels all of the policies like yours in your state. If this happens and you have health problems, you may not be able to qualify medically for another policy. Federal guidelines require that policies be "guaranteed renewable." If your present policy is "conditionally renewable," you should ask an insurance agent about changing to a "guaranteed renewable" policy.

Rating of the Insurance Company—Even if a policy is guaranteed renewable, if the insurance company goes broke, your policy will not stay in force. Buy policies from insurance companies with an A. M. Best Rating of "B+" or higher. Lower ratings (B, C, etc.) put you at risk of losing your policy if the company experiences financial difficulties. See p. 58 for information on how to check an insurance company's ratings and assets.

Pre-existing Conditons—If you replace your old Medicare supplement policy with a new one, the new policy has to cover you immediately for health problems you already have unless the replacement occurs in the first six months after purchasing your first Medicare supplement policy. This means no waiting period for pre-existing conditions for most replacements. If you are just becoming 65 and buying your first Medicare policy, the longest you have to wait for coverage for pre-existing conditions is six months. (See *Open Enrollment* on the following page.)

Underwriting—Unless it is your first policy, Medicare supplement policies you apply for can decline you or charge you more if you have health problems. To get a replacement Medicare supplement policy, you must answer questions about your health. Some companies need time to review your answers and many companies get more information from your doctor. Other companies give your insurance agent the authority to issue you a policy immediately if you can answer "no" to the health questions on the application. In these cases, your agent will leave the policy with you as soon as you complete and sign the application and pay your premium.

Open Enrollment—Federal guidelines guarantee that for six months following enrollment in Part B of Medicare, persons age 65 or older can't be declined or charged more for a Medicare supplement because of health problems. Insurance companies cannot impose a waiting period for pre-existing conditions during the initial open enrollment period if you have had at least six months of health insurance coverage before you apply for the Medicare supplement policy. If you've had less than six months, you get credit for the amount of time you have had health insurance coverage.

On January 1, 1995, federal law extended open enrollment for six months at age 65 to those persons who were first enrolled in Part B of Medicare prior to age 65 by reason of disability or end stage renal disease. If you purchase a Medicare supplement policy as a disabled person prior to age 65, you probably will be able to get Plan A or B. This law means you can get a better policy (Plans C–J) at age 65.

If you or your spouse continue to work past age 65 so that you are covered under an employer's group plan, you can delay enrollment in Part B of Medicare until you are no longer covered under the group plan. When you know your group coverage is ending, you can apply for Part B of Medicare (with no penalty) and you will have the six-month open enrollment period to obtain an individual Medicare supplement policy regardless of any health problems you may have. You will not have a pre-existing waiting period under your new Medicare supplement policy because you will have had health insurance for at least six months prior to the effective date of the Medicare supplement.

Premiums—Many insurance companies allow you to save money if you pay once a year (annually) or twice a year (semi-annually) versus paying monthly or quarterly. If you decide to cancel the policy for any reason, the insurance company does not have to, but may refund the balance of the premiums not used. The three most common methods for premium calculation for Medicare supplement policies are 1) community rating—all policyholders pay the same rate regardless of age, 2) issue age rating—premium is based on the age you apply for the policy and 3) attained age rating—age 65 premium is usually lower than Methods 1 and 2 but increases either annually or in age bands such as every five years as you get older. With Methods 1 and 2, premiums go up only to reflect inflation in the cost of benefits, i.e., as Medicare deductibles and co-payments increase, the policy has to pay out more in benefits so you may see a slight increase from year to year. Method 3 usually has sharper increases as you get older because premiums are actually rising with your age. (A few states, like Missouri, prohibit sales of attained-age policies.)

"Free-Look" Period—You have 30 days after you receive your policy to send it back and get your money back. You can either return it to the agent or send it to the insurance company with a letter saying you do not accept the policy and you wish to have your money returned. Call your state's Department of Insurance if you have any problems getting your money back. (See p. 225.)

Multiple Policies—You don't need more than one Medicare supplement policy. The reason some people have taken out more than one is because they think they can get all of their bills paid if they have more than one policy. This is an unwise use of your money. There are excellent policies on the market today that will take care of most of your expenses with just one policy. Also, federal guidelines don't allow an insurance company to sell you a Medicare supplement policy in addition to one you already have. This means if you buy a new Medicare supplement policy, you agree to cancel the one(s) you already have.

Benefits—An ideal policy will pay both the Part A deductible ($792 per hospital stay in each 60-day benefit period) and the Part B deductible ($100 per calendar year). It will also pay all the coinsurance for additional hospital days and for skilled nursing facility days.

Excess Physician Charges—If your doctor does not accept Medicare assignment, you owe the difference between the actual charge and the amount Medicare approves. However, the doctor can charge no more than 115% of the Medicare-approved amount. Medicare supplement policies are available that will pay these balances. Again, you don't need multiple policies to get these excess charges paid. Plans F, I and J of the standardized plans pay 100% of the excess charges.

Miscellaneous Benefits—Some policies pay extra benefits in addition to Medicare deductibles and coinsurance and excess physician charges. Plans C–J of the standardized plans include at least one of the following extra benefits and Plan J includes all of them.

High Deductible Plans—The Balanced Budget Act of 1997 created a $1,500 deductible option for Plans F and J for policies issued in 1998 and after. The 2001 deductible is

$1,580. This means that covered expenses are paid at 100% after the deductible is met. (The deductible increases each year based on the Consumer Price Index.)

Foreign Travel Emergency —If you become injured or get sick unexpectedly during the first 60 days of a trip outside the United States, the standardized plans C–J will pay 80% of hospital, physician and medical care, subject to a $250 annual deductible and a lifetime maximum of $50,000, if the care would have been covered by Medicare had it been provided in the United States.

Preventive Care—Standardized Plans E and J pay up to $120 per year for such things as an annual physical examination, cholesterol screening, hearing test, diabetes screening and thyroid function test. This benefit can also cover mammograms, Pap smears, and/or flu shots if Medicare stops paying for them.

At Home Recovery—Standardized Plans D, G, I and J pay up to $1,600 per year for short-term, at-home assistance with activities of daily living (bathing, dressing, going to the bathroom, taking medicine, eating, etc.) up to seven visits per week. The visits can last up to four hours and must be received either while you are receiving Medicare-approved home health services or no more than eight weeks after the last Medicare-approved home health visit.

Basic Drugs—Standardized Plans H and I pay 50% of the cost of outpatient prescription drugs up to a maximum annual benefit of $1,250 after a $250 annual deductible. *Extended Drugs*—Standardized Plan J pays the same as the Basic Drugs benefit except the annual maximum is $3,000.

Claims—Medicare supplements usually can't pay unless Medicare pays first. This means that the Medicare supplement insurance company needs to see a copy of the Medicare Explanation of Medical Benefits (EOMB) before processing the claim.

If your doctor participates in the Medicare program (accepts assignment of benefits) and you have assigned the benefits of a qualified Medicare supplement policy to your doctor, the company that processes Medicare claims for your state will automatically send your physician's claim to the Medicare supplement insurance company for processing. You don't have to handle the paperwork of claims processing if your doctor accepts Medicare assignment.

If your doctor does not accept assignment, you are solely responsible for filing your Medicare supplement claims.

Appeals—If you are not satisfied with how the Medicare supplement policy handled your claim, contact the insurance company or your agent. If you are still not satisfied, you can call the Department of Insurance in your state for help. (A list of insurance departments by state starts on p. 227.)

Managed Care for Medicare Supplements

Medicare Select—A new way of handling Medicare supplement insurance was introduced in 1992 in 15 states. In 1995 it was authorized to be sold nationally for three years and approved indefinitely in 1998.

The original Medicare Select states were Alabama, Arizona, California, Florida, Illinois, Indiana, Kentucky, Massachusetts, Minnesota, Missouri, North Dakota, Ohio, Texas, Washington and Wisconsin.

The Medicare Select program allows policyholders to pay a lower premium in return for using a list of hospitals and doctors, called "preferred providers," specified by the insurance company or health maintenance organization (HMO) that underwrites the supplemental policy. The benefits when you use the designated providers are the same as the 10 standard Medicare supplement plans (A–J).

Emergency health care furnished by providers not on the list is also covered. If it's not an emergency and you use a doctor or hospital not on the list, your Medicare supplement claim can be denied or the payment can be reduced. The Medicare benefit is paid as usual, so whether or not you use a health care provider on the list only effects your Medicare supplement benefit, not the Medicare payment.

Call your Department of Insurance for information on Medicare Select plans in your state. (See p. 227.)

Managed Care
Medicare Plans

Managed Care Medicare Plans—In addition to the new Medicare Select plans and the regular Medicare supplement plans, many states have managed care Medicare plans, also called Coordinated Care Plans or HMOs (Health Maintenance Organizations). These plans contract with specific health care providers (hospitals, doctors, skilled nursing facilities, physical therapists, etc.) to provide all the services covered by Medicare. Instead of being responsible for the Medicare deductibles and co-payments, the patient pays the HMO small co-payments (i.e., $5–$15 per doctor visit) and a small monthly premium. Some HMOs do not charge a premium at all. However, you still must pay the $50 monthly Part B premium.

People enrolled in Medicare HMOs don't need a Medicare supplement because all of the services are handled by the HMO, including some preventive services not covered by the traditional Medicare program (prescription drugs, eye and ear exams, dental care, foot care, routine checkups, and so forth).

Depending on the type of plan, the patient either has to receive all non-emergency services from the health care providers on the list to be covered at all or else expect a lower benefit to be paid to providers not on the list. (You may hear the second type referred to as a "point-of-service" option, which just means you pay more out of your pocket to go to a provider outside the HMO's provider network.)

About 17% of people on Medicare belong to a managed care Medicare plan in 1999.[5] Congress is hoping many more people will join because these plans promote cost containment of health care costs. That's why there's little or no premium for those plans and that's why they pay for more services than the traditional Medicare program.

The managed care plans have an annual open enrollment of at least 30 days to allow new enrollees to enter the program. At the present time, people who are enrolled in a managed care plan can go back to the traditional Medicare program at any time.

Some people return to traditional Medicare because managed care plans control how much treatment you can have, and people with chronic conditions sometimes prefer the traditional Medicare program. Rather than lose money on Medicare patients who need a lot of care, some HMOs have stopped serving all Medicare beneficiaries because they feel the government doesn't pay HMOs enough to care for chronically ill patients adequately. That's because the government has been paying managed care plans the same amount of money every month for all Medicare patients in the HMO's geographical service area, regardless of health condition. (When an HMO drops out of Medicare, the members do not lose their Medicare benefits. They just return to the traditional Medicare program.)

Congress has recognized this problem and at some point, Coordinated Care Plans will receive funding based on health conditions as well as geographic area. There's a good chance that the managed care plans that have dropped out may return to the Medicare program when they see the payment system had been adjusted for health conditions.

New Medicare+Choice Plans

By November 1999, you should have received information from the Health Care Financing Administration (HCFA) about several new choices for Medicare beneficiaries who are entitled to Part A and enrolled in Part B of Medicare. (People enrolled in Part B only or with existing end-stage renal disease will continue to be covered by the traditional Medicare program.) These plans are called **Medicare+Choice plans**. The first opportunity for enrollment in one of these new plans was November 1999. If you didn't make a choice, you were left in the traditional Medicare program. But don't worry. You will get another opportunity to enroll in any of the new plans that are available in your area each November.

Enrollment and Disenrollment

To help people become familiar with the new Medicare+Choice plans, there is a phased-in enrollment period. Plans are required to have an "open enrollment," which means any eligible Medicare beneficiary as described above can join, regardless of health conditions, during the month of November each year. Plans also are required to accept people when they first become eligible for Medicare, no questions asked.

In the first few years of this new program, Medicare beneficiaries can disenroll at any time and return to traditional Medicare or switch to another Medicare+Choice plan.

Beginning in 2002, you will only be able to change your enrollment status during the annual open enrollment month of November or during the first six months of 2002. You will be locked in to the plan you have chosen from June–December 2002.

In 2003 and thereafter, you can change your plan only in November or during the first three months of the calendar year.

What Kind of Choices Will You Have?

As this new program develops, there will be several Coordinated Care Plans for you to choose from in addition to the traditional Medicare program, like the HMOs explained earlier. Some of these will require you to use a specific list of providers to receive any benefits, but the benefits you receive will be at little or no cost to you. Others with the "Point of Service" option mentioned on page 216 will allow you to use providers not on the list if you pay more out of your pocket. Other choices include:

Preferred Provider Organizations—You will be given a list of doctors and hospitals to choose from, but you are allowed to use providers not on the list and simply receive lower benefits.

Preferred Sponsor Organizations—This choice allows you to deal directly with the provider of care, such as a particular hospital chain or a group of doctors, without an insurance company's involvement. In other words, the provider is assuming the financial risk of providing services to Medicare patients.

Private fee-for-service plans—These plans do not limit your choice of providers, but are allowed to bill you up to 15% above the plan's payment for a service.

Private contracts with doctors—You will be able to contract privately with doctors who choose to drop out of Medicare for two years. (Contracting privately means you and the doctor agree upon a charge and you can't file the claim with Medicare or a Medicare supplement.)

Religious fraternal benefit societies—Members of these organizations will be able to form their own health care programs.

Another exciting choice is a Medical Savings Account (MSA) for the first 390,000 Medicare beneficiaries who set one up between now and December 31, 2002. An MSA is an exciting choice because it can mean that the government will pay some or maybe even all of your long-term care insurance premium. Here is a brief explanation:

First, you choose a high deductible plan to pay your acute care expenses, like doctor and hospital bills. The maximum deductible in 2000 was $6,300, indexed to increase annually. The government will pay the premium for the acute care plan on a monthly basis. In addition, the government will deposit the difference between the premium for your acute-care plan and the amount the government is providing for each Medicare beneficiary—about $500 per month in 2001, but it could be more depending on where you live—into an account for you. Here's an example using a Medicare allowance of $500 a month:

Medicare's annual allowance ($500 x 12) :	$6,000
Acute-care high deductible plan premium:	- $2,000
Amount Medicare deposits into an account for you	$4,000

This deposit will be made in a lump sum in the first month of your enrollment in the program. Neither the initial deposit nor the growth will be taxable income to you, as long as you use the money for "qualified medical expenses," according to the IRS. That includes expenses that go toward your high deductible, because you aren't allowed to purchase a Medicare supplement to cover that expense. It also includes items beyond what the traditional Medicare program covers such as prescription drugs, eyeglasses, hearing aids, etc.

The really exciting news is that you can also use the money the government has deposited into your MSA for long-term care insurance! Your policy must be tax-qualified. See **Features of a Good Long-Term Care Insurance Policy** on p. 33 for the definition of a tax-qualified policy.

Remember, the Medical Savings Account choice is only available to the first 390,000 people who set one up, so if you are interested, you may want to pursue the idea as soon as one is available in your area. (To find out if a Medical Savings Account choice is available in your area, see *Want to Know More?* p. 222.)

You Do Not Have to Switch

These are all exciting choices, but you do not have to switch to any of these new programs. You may remain in traditional Medicare if you like.

Benefits

All of the Medicare+Choice plans must provide at least the same benefits as Part A and Part B of the traditional Medicare program, including flu shots and pneumonia vaccines and preventive mammograms. Medicare+Choice plans also must:

▲   offer female beneficiaries direct access to specialists for pelvic exams, Pap smears and mammograms without first obtaining a referral from a primary physician;

▲   assess new enrollees to see if they need immediate medical attention of any kind;

▲   allow for direct access to specialists for complex medical conditions; and

▲   pay for diagnostic testing at emergency centers to determine if you need immediate attention and then pay for emergency treatment to stabilize your medical condition for a maximum co-pay of only $50 that you will be responsible for if you need emergency services outside of your plan's provider network. ("Severe pain" is now an accepted medical reason to seek emergency help outside the provider network.)

In addition, Medicare+Choice plans are allowed to include additional benefits that aren't covered by traditional Medicare such as prescription drugs, dental and foot care, and preventive services such as routine physicals and eye and ear exams.

For any services you receive in the new Medicare+Choice plans, your cost sharing is limited to no more than the out-of-pocket costs of the deductibles and co-pays of traditional Medicare and probably will be less.

What If I Don't Like a Medicare+Choice Plan?

Congress passed a safety net in the Balanced Budget Act of 1997 to help people try the new managed care plans. If you try one and don't like it, you can go back to the traditional Medicare program within one year of your enrollment in the managed care plan, and you can get your Medicare supplement policy back "guaranteed issue." This means you can't be turned down or made to wait for pre-existing conditions. People who try a managed care plan as soon as they are eligible for Medicare get the same deal—it's OK if they want to switch to traditional Medicare within one year of enrolling in the new managed care plan, and they can't be turned down if they apply for a Medicare supplement policy when they switch to traditional Medicare.

Want to Know More?

Because the Medicare+Choice program is so new, many areas of the country have only a few, if any, of these selections. For more information on the Medicare+Choice program, you may call 800-633-4227 (TDD-1-877-486-2948) or visit the official Medicare website (www.medicare.gov) to order the publication *Medicare & You, 2001*. In addition to listing a number of valuable publications that you can order or print out to educate yourself thoroughly on Medicare+Choice, the website even allows you to enter your zip code and view a list of Medicare managed care plans available in your area.

The Silver Lining in the Managed Care Opportunity

As you wade through the maze of Medicare changes in the next few years, please bear one thing in mind. The real risk today is long-term care. The average amount spent by Medicare beneficiaries in 1997 for out-of-pocket health expenses was only about $2,149.[6] That amount is much smaller for members of managed care plans, because the government is using lower out-of-pocket costs to create incentives for you to switch from traditional Medicare to managed care. And, the less you spend for your "acute care" coverage like hospital and doctor bills, the more money you have available to spend on long-term care insurance, which covers the greatest health care risk you face and for which you are not covered by Medicare, private health insurance or managed care plans.

Appendix B: Who to Call for Help

Directory of State Insurance Departments, Medicaid and Aging Agencies

ALABAMA

Alabama Insurance Department
Consumer Service Division
135 South Union Street
P. O. Box 303351
Montgomery, AL 36130-3351
(334) 269-3550
Insurance Counseling 1-800-243-5463
(334) 242-5743

Alabama Medicaid Agency
Mr. W. Dale Walley, Acting
Commissioner
501 Dexter Avenue
P. O. Box 5624
Montgomery, AL 36103-5624
(334) 242-5600
(800) 362-1504
Fax Number (334) 242-5097

Commission on Aging
770 Washington Avenue, Suite 470
P. O. Box 301851
Montgomery, AL 36130
1-800-243-5463
(334) 242-5743

ALASKA

Alaska Division of Insurance
3601 C Street, Suite 740
Anchorage, AK 99503
(907) 465-2515
Insurance Counseling (907) 269-7900
1-800-478-6065

Alaska Medicaid Agency
Mr. Robert Labbe, Director
Division of Medical Assistance
Department of Health & Social
Services
P. O. Box 110660
Juneau, AK 99811-0660
(907) 465-3355
Fax Number (907) 465-2204
E-mail: blabbe@health.state.ak.us

Older Alaskans Commission
P.O. Box 110209
Juneau AK 99811-0209
(907) 465-3250

AMERICAN SAMOA

Insurance Department
Office of the Governor
Pago Pago, AS96799
011-684-633-4116

Medicaid Agency
Mr. Niuatoa A. Puletasi
State Medicaid Officer
Department of Health
LBJ Tropical Medical Center
Pago Pago, AS 96799
011-684-633-4590
Fax Number 011-684-633-1869

Territorial Administration on Aging
Government of American Samoa
Pago Pago, AS 96799
011-684-633-1252

ARIZONA

Arizona Insurance Department
2910 N. 44th Street Suite 120
Phoenix, AZ 85018
(602) 912-8444
Insurance Counseling 1-800-432-4040
or (602) 542-6595

Medicaid Agency
Ms. Phyllis Beidess, Director
Arizona Health Care Cost
Containment System
(AHCCCS)
801 East Jefferson Street
Phoenix, AZ 85034
(602) 417-4680
Fax Number (602) 252-6536
E-mail: pxbeidess@ahcccs.state.az.us

Dept. of Economic Security
Aging and Adult Administration
1789 W. Jefferson Street, #950A
Phoenix, AZ 85007
(602) 542-4446

ARKANSAS

Arkansas Insurance Department
Seniors Insurance Network
1123 S. University Avenue, Suite 400
Little Rock, AR 72204
1-800-852-5494
Insurance Counseling (501) 371-2600
or 1-800-852-5494

Medicaid Agency
Mr. Ray Hanley, Director
Division of Medical Services
Department of Human Services
P. O. Box 1437, Slot 1100
Little Rock, AR 72203-1437
(501) 682-8292
TDD: (501) 682-6789
Fax Number (501) 682-1197
E-mail: ray.hanley@medicaid.state.ar.us

Division of Aging and Adult Services
P. O. Box 1437, Slot 1412
Little Rock, AR 72203-1437
(501) 682-2441

Mr. Mark Hemingway
Assistant Director, Office of Long-
Term Care
Division of Medical Services
Department of Human Services
P. O. Box 8059, Slot 400
Little Rock, AR 72203-8059
(501) 682-8487
Fax Number (501) 682-6955

CALIFORNIA

California Insurance Department
300 Capitol Mall, #1500
Sacramento, CA 95814
(916) 445-5544
1-800-927-4357
Insurance Counseling 1-800-927-4357
or (916) 323-7315

Medicaid Agency
Mr. J. Douglas Porter, Deputy
Director
Medical Care Services
Department of Health Services
714 P Street, Room 1253
Sacramento, CA 95814
(916) 654-0391
Fax Number (916) 657-1156
E-mail: dporter@hw1.cahwnet.gov

Department of Aging
Health Insurance Counseling and
Advocacy Branch
1600 K Street
Sacramento, CA 95814
(916) 322-3887
Fax Number(916) 324-1903

COLORADO

Colorado Insurance Division
1560 Broadway
Suite 850
Denver, CO 80202
Insurance Counseling 1-800-544-9181
or (303) 894-7499, ext. 356

Medicaid Agency
Mr. Richard Allen
Executive Director
Dept. of Health Care Policy &
Financing
1575 Sherman Street
Denver, CO 80203-1714
(303) 866-5401
Fax Number (303) 866-2803
TDD (303) 866-3883
E-mail: richard.allen@state.co.us

Division of Aging and Adult Services
Dept. of Social Services
110 16th Street, Suite 200
Denver, CO 80202-5202
(303)620-4147

*COMMONWEALTH OF THE
NORTHERN MARIANA
ISLANDS*

Department of Community &
Cultural Affairs, Civic Center
Commonwealth of the
Northern Mariana Islands
Saipan, CM 96950
011-607-234-6011

Medicaid Agency
Ms. Marcia A.V. Leon Guerrero
Medicaid Administrator
Department of Public Health &
Environmental Services
Commonwealth of the Northern
Mariana Islands
P. O. Box 409 CK
Saipan, MP 96950
011 (670) 664-4880 or 4882
Fax Number 011-670-234-8931

CONNECTICUT

Connecticut Insurance Department
P. O. Box 816
Hartford, CT 06142-0816
(860) 297-3800
Insurance Counseling
1-800-443-9946
(860) 994-9422

Medicaid Agency
Mr. David Parella, Deputy
Commissioner
Department of Social Services
25 Sigourney Street
Hartford, CT 06106-5116
(860) 424-5116
Fax Number (860) 424-5114
E-mail: david.parella@po.state.ct.us

Elderly Services Division
Dept. of Social Services
25 Sigourney Street, 10th Floor
Hartford, CT 06106-5033
(806) 424-5277
1-800-994-9422

DELAWARE

Delaware Insurance Department
Rodney Building
841 Silver Lake Blvd.
Dover, DE 19904
(302) 739-4251
1-800-282-8611
Insurance Counseling 1-800-366-9500
(302) 739-6266

Medicaid Agency
Mr. Philip Soule, Sr., Director
Medical Assistance Program
Department of Health and Social
Services
P. O. Box 906, Lewis Building
1901 North DuPont Highway
New Castle, DE 19720
(302) 577-4901
Fax Number (302) 577-4557
E-mail: PSoule@state.de.us

Division of Services for Aging &
Adults
Dept. of Health & Social Services
1901 N. DuPont Highway
2nd Fl. Annex Admin. Building
New Castle, DE 19720
(302) 577-4791

DISTRICT OF COLUMBIA
Insurance Department
Consumer & Professional Services
Bureau
441 4th Street, NW
Suite 850
Washington, DC 20001
(202) 727-8000 ext. 3041
Insurance Counseling (202) 676-3900

Medicaid Agency
Mr. Herbert H. Weldon, Jr., Deputy
Director
Medical Assistance Administration
Department of Health
825 North Capital St., NE
Fifth Floor
Washington, DC 20002
(202) 442-9090

Office on Aging
441 4th Street, NW
9th Floor
Washington, DC 20001
(202) 724-5626
(202) 724-5622

FEDERATED STATES OF MICRONESIA
State Agency on Aging
Office of Health Services
Federated States of Micronesia
Ponape, ECI 96941

FLORIDA

Florida Department of Insurance
200 E. Gaines Street
Tallahassee, FL 32399-0300
(850) 922-3100
1-800-342-2762
Insurance Counseling (850) 414-2060
or 1-800-963-5337

Medicaid Agency
Mr. Gary Crayton, Director of
Medicaid
Agency for Health Care
Administration
2727 Mahan Drive, Bldg. 3
Tallahassee, FL 32308
(850) 488-3560
Fax Number (850)488-2520

Department of Elder Affairs
Building B-Suite 152
4040 Esplanade Way
Tallahassee, FL 32399-7000
(850) 414-2000
1-800-96ELDER

GEORGIA

Georgia Insurance Department
2 Martin L. King, Jr. Drive
704 West Tower
Atlanta, GA 30334
(404) 656-2070
Insurance Counseling 1-800-669-8387

Medicaid Agency
Mr. Gary B. Redding, Director
Department of Community Health
2 Peachtree Street, NW
Suite 4043
Atlanta, GA 30303-3159
(404) 656-4479
Fax Number (404) 651-6880

Division of Aging Services
Dept. of Human Resources
2 Peachtree St., NW
36-385
Atlanta, GA 30303
(404) 657-5258

GUAM

Guam Insurance Department
Department of Revenue and Taxation
P. O. Box 23607
FMF Barrigada, GU 96921
011-671-475-1825
Insurance Counseling (808) 586-7299

Medicaid Agency
Ms. Ma Theresa Archangel,
Acting Administrator
Bureau of Health Care Financing
Department of Public Health & Social
Services
P. O. Box 2816
Agana, GU 96910
011-671-735-7269
Fax Number 011-671-734-5910

Division of Senior Citizens
Dept. of Public Health & Social
Services
P. O. Box 2816
Agana, GU 96932
011-671-477-2930

HAWAII

Hawaii Dept. of Commerce &
Consumer Affairs
Insurance Division
P. O. Box 3614
Honolulu, HI 96811
(808) 586-2790
Insurance Counseling (808) 586-7299
1-800-586-0100

Medicaid Agency
Mr. Chuck C. Duarte, Administrator
Med-Quest Division
Department of Human Services
P. O. Box 339
Honolulu, HI 96809-0339
(808) 692-8056
Fax Number (808) 692-8173
E-mail: chuck@i-one.com

Executive Office on Aging
No. 1 Capital District
250 S. Hotel Street
Suite 109
Honolulu, HI 96813-2831
(808) 586-0100

IDAHO

Idaho Insurance Department
SHIBA Program
700 W. State St., 3rd Floor
Boise, ID 83720-0043
(208) 334-4350
1-800-721-3272
Insurance Counseling
S.W. 1-800-247-4422
S.E. 1-800-488-5764
N. 1-800-488-5725
C. 1-800-488-5731

Medicaid Agency
Mr. Joe Brunson, Administrator
Division of Medicaid
Department of Health and Welfare
Americana Building
P. O. Box 83720
Boise, ID 83720-0036
(208) 364-1802
Fax Number (208) 364-1811
E-mail: allynkp@mmis.state.id.us

Commission on Aging
700 W. Jefferson, Room 108
Boise, ID 83720-0007
(208) 334-2423

ILLINOIS

Illinois Insurance Department
320 W. Washington St., 4th Floor
Springfield, IL 62767
(217) 782-0004
Insurance Counseling 1-800-252-8966
or (217) 785-9021

Medicaid Agency
Mr. Matt Powers, Administrator
Department of Public Aid
201 South Grand Avenue, East
3rd Floor
Springfield, IL 62763-0001
(217) 782-2570
Fax Number (217) 524-7979
E-mail: aidd0007@mail.idpa.state.il.us

Department on Aging
421 E. Capitol Avenue, No. 100
Springfield, IL 62701-1789
1-800-252-8966
(217) 785-2870

INDIANA

Indiana Insurance Department
311 W. Washington Street, Suite 300
Indianapolis, IN 46204
1-800-622-4461
(317) 232-2395
Insurance Counseling 1-800-452-4800
or (317) 233-3475

Medicaid Agency
Ms. Kathleen D. Gifford, Assistant
Secretary
Medicaid Policy and Planning
Family & Social Services
Administration
Room W383
402 W. Washington Street
Indianapolis, IN 46204-2739
(317) 233-4455
Fax Number (317) 232-7382
Email: KGifford@FSSA.STATE.IN.US

Division of Aging & Home Services
402 W. Washington St.
P. O.Box 7083
Indianapolis, IN 46207-7083
1-800-545-7763
(317) 232-7020

IOWA

Iowa Insurance Division
330 Maple Street
Des Moines, IA 50319-0065
(515) 281-5705
1-800-351-4664
Insurance Counseling 1-800-351-4664
(515) 281-4241

Medicaid Agency
Mr. Dennis Headlee, Administrator
Division of Medical Services
Department of Human Services
Hoover State Office Building
5th Floor
Des Moines, IA 50319-0114
(515) 281-8621
Fax Number (515) 281-7791

Dept. of Elder Affairs
200 10th Street
Third Floor
Des Moines, IA 50309-3709
(515) 281-5187

KANSAS

Kansas Insurance Department
420 S. W. 9th Street
Topeka, KS 66612
(913) 296-3071
1-800-432-2484
Insurance Counseling 1-800-432-3535
(316) 337-7386

Medicaid Agency
Mr. Robert Day, Commissioner
Adult and Medical Services
Department of Social &
Rehabilitation Services
Docking State Office Building
915 Harrison Street
Topeka, KS 66612
(785) 296-8904
Fax Number (785) 296-4813
E-mail: odg@srmspo.wpo.state.ks.us

Department on Aging
New England Bldg.
503 South Kansas
Topeka, KS 66603-3404
(785) 296-4986

KENTUCKY

Kentucky Insurance Department
215 W. Main Street
Frankfort, KY 40602
(502) 564-6034
Insurance Counseling (502) 564-7372
1-800-372-2991

Medicaid Agency
Mr. Dennis Boyd, Commissioner
Department for Medicaid Services
Third Floor
275 East Main Street
Frankfort, KY 40621
(502) 564-4321
Fax Number (502) 564-0509
E-mail: lmccarthy@mail.state.ky.us

Office of Aging Services
Cabinet for Human Resources
275 East Main Street, 5 West
Frankfort, KY 40621
(502) 564-6930

LOUISIANA
Louisiana Insurance Department
P. O. Box 94214
Baton Rouge, LA 70804-9214
1-800-259-5301
(504) 342-5301
Insurance Counseling 1-800-259-5301
(504) 342-0825

Medicaid Agency
Mr. Thomas D. Collins, Director
Bureau of Health Services Financing
Department of Health and Hospitals
P. O. Box 91030
Baton Rouge, LA 70821-9030
(504) 342-3891
Fax Number (504) 342-9508
E-mail: tcollins@dhhmail.dhh-
state.la.us

Office of Elderly Affairs
412 N. 4th Street
P. O. Box 80374
Baton Rouge, LA 70802
(225) 342-7100

MAINE
Maine Bureau of Insurance
34 State House Station
Augusta, ME 04333
(207) 624-8475
1-800-300-5000
Insurance Counseling 1-800-750-5353
(207) 624-5335

Medicaid Agency
Mr. Francis T. Finnegan, Jr., Director
Bureau of Medical Services
Department of Human Services
State House Station 11
Augusta, ME 04333-0011
(207) 287-2093
Fax Number (207) 287-2675
E-mail: fran.finnegan@state.me.us

Bureau of Elder and Adult Services
State House, Station 11
Augusta, ME 04333
(207) 624-5335

MARYLAND

Maryland Insurance Administration
Complaints & Investigation Unit
Life & Health
501 St. Paul Place
Baltimore, MD 21202-2272
(410)767-1270
1-800-492-6116
Insurance Counseling 1-800-243-3425
or (410)767-1100

Medicaid Agency
Ms. Debbie Chang, Deputy Secretary
for Health Care Financing
Department of Health and Mental
Hygiene
201 West Preston Street
Baltimore, MD 21201
(410) 767-4664
Fax Number (410) 333-7687
E-mail: dchang@dhmh.md.state.us

Department on Aging
301 W. Preston Street
Room 1004
Baltimore, MD 21201
(410) 767-1100

MASSACHUSETTS

Massachusetts Insurance Division
Consumer Services Section
470 Atlantic Avenue
Boston, MA 02210-2223
(617) 521-7777
Insurance Counseling 1-800-882-2003
or (617) 727-7750

Medicaid Agency
Mr. Bruce Bullen, Commissioner
Division of Medical Assistance
600 Washington Street
Boston, MA 02111
(617) 210-5690
Fax Number (617) 210-5697
E-mail: bbullen@nt.dma.state.ma.us

Executive Office of Elder Affairs
1 Ashburton Place, 5th Floor
Boston, MA 02108
1-800-882-2003
(617) 727-7750

MICHIGAN

Michigan Insurance Bureau
P. O. Box 30220
Lansing, MI 48909
(517) 373-0240 (General Assistance)
(517) 335-1702 (Senior Issues)
Insurance Counseling (517) 373-8230
1-800-803-7174

Medicaid Agency
Mr. Robert M. Smedes
Chief Executive Officer
Medical Services Administration
Department of Community Health
400 S. Pine Street
Lansing, MI 48909
(517) 335-5001
Fax Number (517) 335-5007
E-mail: smedes@state.mi.us

Office of Services to the Aging
P. O. Box 30676
Lansing, MI 48909-8176
(517) 373-8230

MINNESOTA

Minnesota Insurance Department
Department of Commerce
133 E. 7th Street
St. Paul, MN 55101-2362
(612) 296-2488
Insurance Counseling 1-800-882-6262

Medicaid Agency
Ms. Mary B. Kennedy, Medicaid
Director
Assistant Commissioner Health Care
Minnesota Department of Human
Services
444 Lafayette Road
St. Paul, MN 55155-3852
(651) 282-9921
Fax Number (651) 297-3230
E-mail: mary.kennedy@state.mn.us

Board on Aging
444 Lafayette Road
St. Paul, MN 55155-3843
(651) 296-2770

MISSISSIPPI

Mississippi Insurance Department
Consumer Assistance Division
P. O. Box 79
Jackson, MS 39205
(601) 359-2130
1-800-562-2957
Insurance Counseling (601) 359-4929
1-800-948-3090

Medicaid Agency
Ms. Anna Marie Barnes, Acting
Director
Division of Medicaid
Office of the Governor
Suite 801, Robert E. Lee Building
239 North Lamar Street
Jackson, MS 39201-1399
(601) 359-6050
Fax Number (601) 359-6048
E-mail: exhaw@medicaid.state.ms.us

Council on Aging & Adult Services
750 N. State Street
Jackson, MS 39202
1-800-948-3090
(601) 359-4929

MISSOURI

Missouri Department of Insurance
Consumer Assistance Division
P. O. Box 690
Jefferson City, MO 65102-0690
1-800-726-7390
(573) 751-4126
Insurance Counseling 1-800-390-3330
or (573) 893-7900

Medicaid Agency
Mr. Gregory A. Vadner
Division of Medical Services
Department of Social Services
615 Howerton Court
P. O. Box 6500
Jefferson City, MO 65102-6500
(573) 751-6922
Fax Number (573) 751-6564
E-mail: victornine@aol.com

Division of Aging
Department of Social Services
P.O. Box 1337
615 Howerton Court
Jefferson City, MO 65102-1337
(573) 751-3082

MONTANA

Montana Insurance Department
126 N. Sanders
Mitchell Building, Room 270
P. O. Box 4009
Helena, MT 59601
(406) 444-2040
1-800-332-6148
Insurance Counseling (406) 444-7781
1-800-332-2272

Medicaid Agency
Ms. Nancy Ellery, Administrator
Division of Health Policy and Services
Department of Public Health &
Human Services
1400 Broadway
Helena, MT 59601
(406) 444-4141
Fax Number (406) 444-1861
E-mail: nellery@state.mt.us

Senior & Long-Term Care Dvision
111 Sanders Street
P. O. Box 4210
Helena, MT 59604
1-800-332-2272
(406) 444-4077

NEBRASKA

Nebraska Insurance Department
Terminal Building
941 "0" Street, Suite 400
Lincoln, NE 68508
(402) 471-2201
Insurance Counseling (402) 471-4506

Medicaid Agency
Cec Brady, Interim Administration
Medicaid Division
Nebraska Dept. of HHS Finance &
Support
P.O. Box 95026
Lincoln, NE 68509-5026
(402) 471-9506
Fax Number (402) 471-9092

Department on Aging
State Office Building
301 Centennial Mall South
Lincoln, NE 68509-5044
(402) 471-2306

NEVADA

Nevada Department of Business &
Industry
Division of Insurance
1665 Hot Springs Road, Suite 152
Carson City, NV 89710
(775)687-4270
(800) 992-0900
Insurance Counseling (702) 486-4602
1-800-307-4444

Medicaid Agency
Ms. Mary Wherry, Administrator
Nevada State Welfare Division
2527 North Carson Street
Carson City, NV 89710
(775) 687-6667
Fax Number (775) 687-5080

Department of Health & Human
Services
Division for Aging Services
340 North 11th Street, Suite 203
Las Vegas, NV 89101
(702) 486-3545

Mr. Phil Nowack, Administrator
Division of Health Care Financing &
Policy
1100 East William Street, Suite 119
Carson City, NV 89710
(775) 687-4176 ext. 228
Fax Number (775) 684-8792
E-mail: pnowak@govmail.state.nv.us

NEW HAMPSHIRE

New Hampshire Insurance
Department
Life & Health Division
169 Manchester Street
Concord, NH 03301
(603) 271-2261
1-800-852-3416
Insurance Counseling 1-800-852-3388
(603) 271-4642

Medicaid Agency
Ms. Lee Bezanson
Medicaid Director
Medicaid Administration Bureau
Department of Health and Human
Services
6 Hazen Drive
Concord, NH 03301-6521
(603) 271-4353
Fax Number (603) 271-4376

Dept. of Health & Human Services
Division of Elderly & Adult Services
State Office Park South
115 Pleasant Street
Annex Building No. 1
Concord, NH 03301
(603) 271-4394

NEW JERSEY
New Jersey Insurance Department
20 West State Street
Roebling Building
CN 325
Trenton, NJ 08625
(609) 292-5360
Insurance Counseling 1-800-792-8820

Medicaid Agency
Ms. Margaret A. Murray, Director
Division of Medical Assistance &
Health Services
Department of Human Services
P.O. Box 712
Trenton, NJ 08625-0712
(609) 588-2600
Fax Number (609) 588-3583

Department of Community Affairs
Division on Aging
101 South Broad Street
CN 807
Trenton, NJ 08625-0807
1-800-792-8820
(609) 984-3951

NEW MEXICO
New Mexico Insurance Department
P. O. Drawer 1269
Santa Fe, NM 87504-1269
(505) 827-7640
1-800-947-4722
Insurance Counseling 1-800-432-2080
(505)827-7640

Medicaid Agency
Mr. Charles J. Milligan, Director
Medical Assistance Division
New Mexico Human Services
Department
P. O. Box 2348
Santa Fe, NM 87504-2348
(505) 827-3100
1-888-997-2583 Toll free
client information
Fax Number (505) 827-3185
E-mail: charles.milligan@state.nm.us

State Agency on Aging
La Villa Rivera Building
228 East Palace Avenue, Ground Floor
Santa Fe, NM 87501
1-800-432-2080 or (505) 827-7640

NEW YORK

New York Insurance Department
25 Beaver Street
New York, NY 10004
(212) 480-2312
1-800-342-3736
Outside of New York City
1-800-342-3736
Insurance Counseling 1-800-333-4114
(212) 869-3850—NY City Area

Medicaid Agency
Ms. Kathryn Kuhmerker
Deputy Commissioner
NYS Department of Health
Office of Medicaid Management
Empire State Plaza
Room 1466, Corning Tower Building
Albany, NY 12237
(518) 474-3018
Fax Number (518) 486-6652
E-mail: dbf02@health.state.ny.us

State Office for the Aging
New York State Plaza Agency
Building #2
Albany, NY 12223-0001
1-800-342-9871
(518) 474-5731

NORTH CAROLINA

North Carolina Insurance Department
Seniors' Health Insurance Information
Program (SHIIP)
P. O. Box 26387
Raleigh, NC 27611
(919) 733-0111 (SHIIP)
1-800-662-7777 (Consumer Services)
Insurance Counseling 1-800-443-9354
(919) 733-0111

Medicaid Agency
Mr. Paul R. Perruzzi, Director
Division of Medical Assistance
Department of Health and Human
Services
1985 Umstead Drive
P. O. Box 29529
Raleigh, NC 27626-0529
(919) 857-4011
Fax Number (919) 733-6608
E-mail: dick.perruzzi@ncmail.net

Division of Aging
CB 29531
693 Palmer Drive
Raleigh, NC 27626-0531
(919) 733-0443

NORTH DAKOTA

North Dakota Insurance Department
Senior Health Insurance Counseling
600 East Boulevard
Bismarck, ND 58505-0320
1-800-247-0560
(701) 328-2440
Insurance Counseling 1-800-247-0560
(701) 328-2977

Medicaid Agency
Mr. David J. Zentner, Director
Division of Medical Assistance
Department of Human Services
600 East Boulevard Avenue
Bismarck, ND 58505-0261
(701) 328-3194
Fax Number (701) 328-1544
E-mail: sozend@state.nd.us

Dept. of Human Services
Aging Services Division
600 South 2nd Street, Suite 1C
Bismarck, ND 58504
(701) 328-8909
1-800-755-8521

OHIO

Ohio Insurance Department
Consumer Services Division
2100 Stella Court
Columbus, OH 43215-1067
(614) 644-3376
1-800-686-1526
Insurance Counseling 1-800-686-1578
or (614) 644-3458

Medicaid Agency
Ms. Barbara Edwards, Acting Deputy
Director
Office of Medicaid
Department of Human Services
30 East Broad Street
31st Floor
Columbus, OH 43266-0423
(614) 644-0140
Fax Number (614) 752-3986
E-mail: medicaid@odhs.state.oh.us

Department of Aging
50 W. Broad Street
9th Floor
Columbus, OH 43215-5928
(614) 466-5500
1-800-282-1206

OKLAHOMA

Oklahoma Insurance Department
P. O. Box 53408
Oklahoma City, OK 73152-3408
(405) 521-6628
1-800-522-0071
Insurance Counseling (405) 521-6628
1-800-763-2828

Medicaid Agency
Mr. Michael Fogarty
State Medicaid Director
Oklahoma Health Care Authority
4545 North Lincoln Boulevard,
Suite 124
Oklahoma City, OK 73105
(405) 522-7373
Fax Number (405) 530-3478
E-mail: fogartym@ohca.state.ok.us

Department of Human Services
Aging Services Division
312 NE 28th Street
Oklahoma City, OK 73125
(405) 521-2327

OREGON

Oregon Dept. of Consumer &
Business Services
Senior Health Insurance Benefits
Assistance
350 Winter Street, N.E., Room 440
Salem, OR 97310
(503) 378-4100
1-800-722-4134
Insurance Counseling 1-800-722-4134
or (503) 947-7250

Medicaid Agency
Mr. Hersh Crawford, Director
Senior and Disabled Services Division
Department of Human Resources
500 Summer Street, N.E.,
Salem, OR 97310-1015
(503) 945-5767
Fax Number (503) 373-7689
E-mail: herschel.crawford@state.or.us

Department of Human Resources
Senior & Disabled Services Division
500 Summer Street, NE, 2nd Floor
Salem, OR 97310-1015
1-800-232-3020
(503) 945-5811

PALAU
State Agency on Aging
Department of Social Services
Republic of Palau
P.O. Box 100
Koror, Palau 96940

PENNSYLVANIA
Pennsylvania Insurance Department
Consumer Services Bureau
1321 Strawberry Square
Harrisburg, PA 17120
(717) 787-2317
Insurance Counseling 1-800-783-7067
(717) 783-8975

Medicaid Agency
Margaret J. Dierkers, Ph.D.
Deputy Secretary
Medical Assistance Programs
Department of Public Welfare
Health and Welfare Building,
Room 515
Harrisburg, PA 17120
(717) 787-1870
Fax Number (717) 787-4639
E-mail: pamedicaid2@dpw.state.pa.us

Department of Aging
"APPRISE" Health Insurance
Counseling & Assistance
400 Market Street
Rachel Carson State Office Building
Harrisburg, PA 17101
1-800-783-7067

PUERTO RICO
Office of the
Commissioner of Insurance
P. O. Box 8330
San Juan, PR 00910-8330
(809) 722-8686
Insurance Counseling (787) 721-8590
1-800-981-4355

Medicaid Agency
Ms. Margarita Latorre, Medicaid
Director
Office of Economic Assistance to the
Medically Indigent—Department of
Health
G.P.O. Box 70184
San Juan, PR 00936
(809) 765-1230
Fax Number (809) 250-0990

Governor's Office of Elderly Affairs
P.O. Box 50063
Old San Juan Station
San Juan, PR 00902
(787) 721-5710

REPUBLIC OF THE MARSHALL ISLANDS
State Agency on Aging
Department of Social Services
Republic of the Marshall Islands
Marjuro, Marshall Islands 96960

RHODE ISLAND

Rhode Island Insurance Division
233 Richmond Street, Suite 233
Providence, RI 02903-4233
(401) 421-0172
Insurance Counseling 1-800-322-2880
(401) 222-2880

Medicaid Agency
Mr. John Young, C.P.M.
Associate Director
Division of Medical Services
Department of Human Services
600 New London Avenue
Cranston, RI 02920
(401) 464-3113
Fax Number (401) 462-6338
E-mail: jyoung@gw.dhs.state.ri.us

Dept. of Elderly Affairs
160 Pine Street
Providence, RI 02903-3708
(401) 222-2858

SOUTH CAROLINA

South Carolina Department of
Insurance
Consumer Services Section
P. O. Box 100105
Columbia, SC 29202-3105
(803) 737-6150
1-800-768-3467
Insurance Counseling 1-800-868-9095
or (803) 253-6177

Medicaid Agency
Dr. J. Samuel Griswald, Ph.D.
Director
Department of Health and Human
Services
P. O. Box 8206
Columbia, SC 29202-8206
(803) 898-2504
Fax Number (803) 898-4515
E-mail: griswald@dhhs.state.sc.us

Division on Aging
202 Arbor Lake Drive
Suite 301
Columbia, SC 29223-4554
(803) 737-7500

SOUTH DAKOTA

South Dakota Insurance Department
500 East Capitol Avenue
Pierre, SD 57501-5070
(605) 773-3563
Insurance Counseling (605) 773-3656
or 1-800-822-8804

Medicaid Agency
Mr. David M. Christensen
Program Administrator Medical
Services
Department of Social Services
Richard F. Kneip Building
700 Governors Drive
Pierre, SD 57501-2291
(605) 773-3495
Fax Number (605) 773-5246
E-mail: dave.christensen@state.sd.us

Office of Adult Services and Aging
700 Governors Drive
Pierre, SD 57501-2291
(605) 773-3656

TENNESSEE

Tennessee Department of Commerce
& Insurance
Insurance Assistance Office
4th Floor
500 James Robertson Pkwy
Nashville, TN 37243
1-800-342-4029
(615) 741-4955
Insurance Counseling 1-800-525-2816
(615) 741-4955

Medicaid Agency
Mr. John F. Tighe, Deputy
Commissioner
Dept. of Finance and Administration
729 Church Street
Nashville, TN 37247-6501
(615) 741-0213
Fax Number (615) 741-0882
E-mail: blapps@mail.state.tn.us

Commission on Aging
Andrew Jackson Building
9th Floor
500 Deaderick Street
Nashville, TN 37243-0860
(615) 741-2056

TEXAS

Texas Department of Insurance
Complaints Resolution, MC 111-1A
333 Guadalupe Street (78701)
P. O. Box 149091
Austin, TX 78714-9091
(512) 463-6169
1-800-252-3439
Insurance Counseling 1-800-252-3439
(512) 424-6840

Medicaid Agency
Ms. Linda K. Wertz
State Medicaid Director
Health and Human Services
Commission
P. O. Box 13247
Austin, TX 78711
(512) 424-6549
Fax Number (512) 424-6547
E-mail: linda.wertz@hhsc.state.tx.us

Department on Aging
4900 North Lamar
4th Floor
Austin, TX 78751-2316
(512) 424-6840
1-800-252-9240

UTAH

Utah Insurance Department
Consumer Services
3110 State Office Building
Salt Lake City, UT 84114-6901
1-800-439-3805
(801) 538-3805
Insurance Counseling (801) 538-3910
1-800-439-3805

Medicaid Agency
Mr. Rod Betit, Executive Director
Department of Health
Division of Health Care Financing
P. O. Box 14100
Salt Lake City, UT 84114-1000
(801) 538-6111
Fax Number (801) 538-6306

Division of Aging & Adult Services
120 North 200 West
Salt Lake City, UT 84103
(801) 538-3910
1-800-606-0608

VERMONT

Vermont Department of Banking
& Insurance
Consumer Complaint Division
89 Main Street, Drawer 20
Montpelier, VT 05620-3101
(802) 828-3301
Insurance Counseling 1-800-642-5119

Medicaid Agency
Mr. Paul Wallace-Brodeur, Acting
Director
Office of Health Access
Department of Social Welfare
103 South Main Street
Waterbury, VT 05671
(802) 241-3985
Fax Number (802) 241-2974
E-mail: paulw@wpgate1.ahs.state.vt.us

Aging & Disabilities
Waterbury Complex
103 South Main Street
Waterbury, VT 05671-2301
(802) 241-2325

VIRGINIA

Virginia Bureau of Insurance
1300 E. Main Street
Richmond, VA 23219
(804) 371-9074
1-800-552-7945
Insurance Counseling 1-800-552-4464
(804) 662-9333

Medicaid Agency
Mr. Dennis G. Smith, Director
Department of Medical Assistance
Services
600 East Broad Street, Suite 1300
Richmond, VA 23219
(804) 786-8099
Fax Number (804) 371-4981
E-mail: dsmith@dmas.state.va.us

Dept. for the Aging
1600 Forest Avenue
Preston Building, Suite 102
Richmond, VA 23229
1-800-552-4464
(804) 662-9354

VIRGIN ISLANDS
Virgin Islands Insurance Department
Kongens Gade No. 18
St. Thomas, VI 00802
(809) 774-2991
Insurance Counseling
(340) 774-7166

Medicaid Agency
Ms. Priscilla Berry-Quetel, Director
Bureau of Health Insurance and
Medical Assistance
Department of Health
210-3A Altona
Suite 302 Frostco Center
Charlotte Amalie, VI 00802
(809) 774-4624
Fax Number (809) 774-4918

Senior Citizen Affairs Division
Department of Human Services
19 Estate Diamond Fredericksted
St. Croix, VI 00840
(340) 692-5950

WASHINGTON
Washington Insurance Department
4224 6th Avenue, SE, Building 4
P. O. Box 40256
Lacey, WA 98504-0256
1-800-562-6900
(360) 753-7300
Insurance Counseling 1-800-397-4422
(206) 654-1833

Medicaid Agency
Mr. Tom Bedell, Acting Assistant
Secretary
Medical Assistance Administration
P. O. Box 45080
Olympia, WA 98504-5080
(360) 902-7802
Fax Number (360)902-7855
E-mail: bedeltw@dshs.wa.gov

Aging & Adult Services
Administration
Department of Social & Health
Services
P. O. Box 45600
Olympia, WA 98504-5050
(360) 902-7797

WEST VIRGINIA

West Virginia Insurance Department
Consumer Services
P. O. Box 50540
Charleston, WV 25305-0540
(304) 558-3386
1-800-642-9004
1-800-435-7381 (hearing impaired)
Insurance Counseling (304) 558-3317
or 1-800-642-9004

Medicaid Agency
Ms. Elizabeth Lawton, Commissioner
Bureau for Medical Services
Department of Health & Human
Resources
7011 MacCorkle Avenue, SE
Charleston, WV 25304
(304) 926-1703 (Secretary)
Fax Number (304) 926-1833
E-mail: elawton@wvdhhr.org

WV Bureau of Senior Services
1900 Kanawha Blvd, East
Holly Grove—Building 10
Charleston, WV 25305-0160
(304) 558-0004

WISCONSIN

Wisconsin Insurance Department
Complaints Department
P. O. Box 7873
Madison, WI 53707
1-800-236-8517
(608) 266-0103
Insurance Counseling 1-800-242-1060
(608) 267-3201

Medicaid Agency
Ms Peggy Bartels, Administrator
Division of Health Care Financing
Department of Health & Social
Services
One West Wilson Street
Room 350
Madison, WI 53701
(608) 266-8922
Fax Number (608) 266-1096
E-mail: bartepl@dhfs.state.wi.us

Board on Aging and LTC Resources
217 South Hamilton Street, Suite 300
Madison, WI 53703
(608) 266-2536
1-800-242-1060

WYOMING
Wyoming Insurance Department
Herschler Building, 3E
122 West 25th Street
Cheyenne, WY 82002
1-800-438-5768
(307) 777-7402
Insurance Counseling 1-800-438-5768
(307) 856-6880

Medicaid Agency
Mr. Daniel D. Stackis, Administrator
Health Care Access & Resources
Divison
Department of Health
Hathaway Building, Suite 154
2300 Capitol Avenue
Cheyenne, WY 82002
(307) 777-7531
Fax Number (307) 777-6964
E-mail: rdavis@state.wy.us
or iolesk@state.wy.us

WDH Division on Aging
Hathaway Building
2300 Capitol Avenue, Room 139
Cheyenne, WY 82002-0710
1-800-442-2766
(307) 777-7986

Useful Web Sites

The following is a list of web sites that we at *LTC Consultants* have found to be helpful. We feel that these web sites can be useful to anyone who wants to learn more about long-term care and long-term care insurance.

American Association of Homes and Services for the Aging: www.aahsa.org

American Association of Retired Persons: www.aarp.org

American Psychological Association: www.apa.org

Careguide: www.careguide.com

Caregiver Zone: www.caregiverzone.com

Center for Long-Term Care Financing: www.centerltc.com

ElderCare Online: www.ec-online.net

e-Eldercare: www.e-eldercare.com

ElderWeb Online Eldercare Sourcebook: www.elderweb.com

Federal Administration on Aging: www.aoa.gov

LTC Consultants: www.ltcconsultants.com

The Medicine Program: www.themedicineprogram.com

Mr. Long-Term Care: www.mrltc.com

National Alliance for Caregiving: www.caregiver.org

National Senior Citizen's Law Center: www.nsclc.org

National Association of Social Workers: www.socialworkers.org

National Family Caregivers Association: www.nfcacares.org

NJ Self-Help Clearinghouse: www.njshc.org

Official Medicare Web Site: www.medicare.gov

Senior Alternatives: www.senioralternatives.com

Well Spouse Foundation: www.wellspouse.org

Adult Day Care

The Administration of Aging's Adult Day Care Resources: www.aoa.dhhs.aoa/webres/adultday.htm

National Adult Day Services Association: www.ncoa.org/nadsa/nadsa.html

Assisted Living Facilities

Assisted Living Federation of America: www.alfa.org

Assisted Living Info: www.assistedlivinginfo.com

Consumer Consortium on Assisted Living: www.ccal.org

National Center for Assisted Living: www.ncal.org

Home Health Care

HOMECARE Online: www.nahc.org
Web site of the National Association for Home Care.

Visiting Nurse Associations of America: www.vnaa.org

Nursing Homes

Nursing Home Compare, National Nursing Home Database from the Health Care Financing Administration: www.medicare.gov/nursing/home.asp

Nursing Home Info, Nationwide Nursing Home Directory: www.nursinghomeinfo.com

Senior Care Resources, Nursing Home Report Cards Online: www.seniorcarehelp.com

Alzheimer's Information

Alzheimer's Assocation: www.alz.org
Alzheimers.com, published by PlanetRx: www.alzheimers.com

Appendix C:
Sources

Sources for Introduction:

1. The Urban Institute/The Congressional Research Service, 2000

2. **AgePower**, Dychtwald, 1999

3. The Conference Board, 1997 / *Business Insurance*, 1996

Sources for Chapter 1:
Long-Term Care and Your Financial Security

1. Miller, Jessica, "The Changing Face of Long-Term Care," *CARING* Magazine, August 1998, p. 24

2. "2000 Nursing Home Cost Survey" MetLife Mature Market Institute, Released July 24, 2000. (Nursing home costs include semi-private room rate plus an estimated 20% for miscellaneous charges, such as prescription drugs and care-related supplies)

3. "2000 Home Health Care Cost Survey", MetLife Mature Market Institute, Released July 24, 2000.

4. "2000 Nursing Home Cost Survey" and "2000 Home Health Care Cost Survey", MetLife Mature Market Institute, Released July 24, 2000.

5. *Projected Needs of the Aging Baby Boomers,* General Accounting Office, 6/91, GAO/HRD-91-86, p.12 (Supported by Health Care Financing Administration's current projection of 5.8% for 1993–2008 in "The Next Decade of Health Spending: A New Outlook," *Health Affairs*, July/August 1999, p. 93)

6. Nashville, Tennessee annual cost surveys 1990-2001 provided by John Hancock Financial Services, Nashville, Tennessee

7. *The Caregiving Boom: Baby Boomer Women Giving Care*, National Alliance For Caregiving, September 1998, p. 8

8. "The National Nursing Home Survey: 1997 Summary", Table 25, P. 28, National Center for Health Statistics

9. Dychtwald, Ken, PhD, **Healthy Aging: Challenges and Solutions**, Aspen Publishers, 1999, p. 8

10. "Statistical Data on Alzheimer's Disease," Alzheimer's Association, 2000

11. Koppel, Ross PhD, "Alzheimer's Cost to U.S. Business," Alzheimer's Association, September 1998

12. *Family Caregiving in the U.S., Findings from a National Survey*, AARP/National Alliance for Caregiving, 1997

13. "1999 Long-Term Care Survey," National Council on Aging/John Hancock, p. 2

14. Franklin, Mary Beth, "Knowing the Score," *Kiplinger's Personal Finance Magazine*, March 2000, p. 95

15. *Who Buys Long-Term Care Insurance? 1994-1995 Profiles and Innovations in a Dynamic Market*, Health Insurance Association of America/Life Plans, Inc., p. 2 (Confirmed with LifePlans, Inc., January 2001)

16. Brown, Dr. Robert, associate professor of neurology, Mayo Medical School, Mayo Clinic, Rochester, Minnesota, February, 2000

17. Dychtwald, Ken PhD, **Healthy Aging: Challenges and Solutions,** Aspen Publishers, 1999, p. 199

18. *1999 Data Compendium*, Health Care Financing Administration, p. 55

19. *Demography Is Not Destiny*, National Academy on an Aging Society, a policy institute of The Gerontological Society of America, January 1999, p. 55

20. "Centenarians in the United States," Census Bureau, July 1999 p.2

21. "Minor Memos," *Wall Street Journal*, December 31, 1999, p. 1

22. Friend, Tim, "Science Finds No Limit on Life Span," *USA Today*, March 17, 1999

23. *Wall St. Journal*, December 26, 1997

24. Manton, Kenneth G. and Stallard, Eric, "Longevity in the United States: Age and Sex-Specific Evidence on Life Span Limits from Mortality Patterns 1960-1990," Center for Demographic Studies, Duke University, *The Journals of Gerontology: Biological and Medical Sciences*, September 1996

25. Laditka, Sarah B., "Modeling Lifetime Nursing Home Use Under Assumptions of Better Health," *The Journals of Gerontology: Psychological and Social Sciences*, July 1998, pp. S177-S187

26. Urrea, Yvette, "Friends of Paralyzed Surfer Set Up Fund," *North County Times,* March 31, 2000, pp. A1, A9

27. Tilly, Jane, et al, "Long-Term Care Chart Book: Persons Served, Payors, and Spending," The Urban Institute in Collaboration with the Congressional Research Service, May 5, 2000, p. 12

28. *Facts and Trends,* "The Nursing Facility Sourcebook," American Health Care Association, 1999, p. 6

29. "Traumatic Brain Injury: Programs Supporting Long-Term Care Services in Selected States," General Accounting Office, February 1998, GAO/HEHS-98-55, pp. 1, 4.

30. Schrop, Joannie M., "Stroke Busters: New Treatments in the Fight Against Brain Attacks," *U.S. News & World Report,* March 15, 1999, p. 62

31. Penning, Margaret J., "In the Middle: Parental Caregiving in the Context of Other Roles," *The Journals of Gerontology: Psychological and Social Sciences,* July 1998, pp. S188–S197

32. Bureau of Labor Statistics, February 2001

33. Dychtwald, Ken, PhD, **AgePower,** Penguin Putnam, Inc. Publishers, 1999, p. 146

34. Prince, Michael, "Elder Care Benefits Valued: Demand for Benefit Expected to Grow," *Business Insurance,* July 29, 1996, p. 3

35. National Council on Aging/John Hancock Long-Term Care Survey, 1999

36. Saluter, Arlene F. and Lugaila, Terry A., "Marital Status and Living Arrangements: March 1998," Current Population Reports, Census Bureau Report P20-496/PPL-100 (Update)

37. Carter, Jessica. "Workshop to Help Those Who Care for Loved Ones," *Daily News Journal*, Murfreesboro, Tennessee, April 18, 2000, p. 1B

38. Krauss, N.A., Altman, B.M. "Characteristics of nursing home residents—1996." Rockville (MD): Agency for Health Care Policy and Research; 1998 MEPS Research Findings No. 5. AHCPR Pub. No. 99-0006

39. Spillman, Brenda C and Pezzin, Liliana E., *"Potential and Active Family Caregivers: Changing Networks and the 'Sandwich Generation'"*, The Urban Institute; John Hopkins University School of Medicine, *The Milbank Quarterly*, Vol. 78, No. 3, 2000

40. *Contra Costa Times*, Walnut Creek, California, March 29, 1996, Reporter: Julie Appleby

41. *Parade Magazine*, March 1, 1998

42. Meyers, Bill, "It's a Small Business World", *USA Today*, July 30, 1999, p. 2B and Mergenhagen, Paula, "Her Own Boss," *American Demographics*, December 1996, P. 37

43. *Family Caregiving in the U.S., Findings from a National Study,* National Alliance for Caregiving/AARP, 1997, p. 33

44. Schrop, Joannie M., "Stroke Busters: New Treatments in the Fight Against Brain Attacks," *U.S. News & World Report,* March 15, 1999

45. Health Care Financing Administration, 1998 statistics

46. *Contra Costa Times,* Walnut Creek, California, March 29, 1996, Reporter: Julie Appleby

47. Health Care Financing Administration, "Table 38: Use of Skilled Nursing Facility Services by Medicare Hospital Insurance Beneficiaries: Number of Covered Admissions, Covered Days of Care, Covered Charges, and Reimbursement by Region, Division and State," 1998

48. Health Care Financing Administration, 1998 statistics

49. Spillman, Brenda C., PhD and Kemper, Peter PhD, "Lifetime Patterns of Payment for Nursing Home Care," Agency for Health Care Policy and Research, as published in *Medical Care,* Vol. 33, No. 3, 1995, p. 291 and Wiener, Joshua M., Sullivan, Catherine M. and Skaggs, Jason, The Brookings Institution, "Spending Down to Medicaid: New Data on the Role of Medicaid in Paying for Nursing Home Care," as published by *AARP, The Public Policy Institute,* June 1996, p. 21.

50. Health Care Financing Administration, 1998 statistics

51. *Demography Is Not Destiny*, National Academy on an Aging Society, a policy institute of The Gerontological Society of America, January 1999, p. 11.

52. "The Public Policy and Aging Report," National Academy on an Aging Society, Summer 1999, p. 11.

53. A conservative estimate based on historical growth and number of existing policies documented in *Long-Term Care Insurance in 1997–1998*, Coronel, Susan, Health Insurance Association of America, March 2000

54. Ash, Patricia E., *U.S. Group Long-Term Care Insurance: 1999 Sales and In Force*, Life Insurance Market Research Association (LIMRA), 2000

55. Health Care Financing Administration, 1998 statistics

56. Coronel, Susan, "Buyers and Non-Buyers of Long-Term Care Insurance," presented to the 14th Private Long-Term Care Insurance Conference, Monterey, CA, June 26-28, 2000, Health Insurance Association of America/Life Plans, Inc.

57. *Ibid*

58. "A Health Care Safety Net," *Fortune*, Kuhn, Susan E., October 14, 1996, p. 299

59. "Out-of-Pocket Health Care Costs Among Older Americans," *The Journals of Gerontology: Psychological and Social Sciences*, January 2000, Volume 55B, No. 1, p. S51

60. "Living Longer and Better, Long-Term Care: A Crucial Piece of the Retirement Puzzle," *Fortune*, October 1998 Special Investor's Issue, p. S3

61. Vanac, Mary, "Plan Now for Later," *Akron Beacon Journal*, August 30, 1999

62. Chatzky, Jean Sherman, "The Big Squeeze," *Money*, October 1999, p. 138

Sources for Chapter 2:
Features of a Good Long-Term Care Insurance Policy

1. Rhoades, J.A., Krauss, N.A. "Nursing Home Trends, 1987 and 1996." Rockville (MD): Agency for Health Care Policy and Research, 1999, MEPS Chartbook No. 3, AHCRP Pub. No. 99-0032, pp. 6, 12

2. *The Assisted Living Industry 1999: An Overview,* Assisted Living Federation of America and *Basic Statistics about Home Care*, National Association for Home Care, 1999

3. Assisted Living Federation of America, 1999

4. Health Care Financing Administration, 1998 statistics

5. *The Assisted Living Industry 1999: An Overview*, Assisted Living Federation of America, 1999

6. "2000 Nursing Home Cost Survey" MetLife Mature Market Institute, Released July 24, 2000. (Nursing home costs include semi-private room rate plus an estimated 20% for miscellaneous charges, such as prescription drugs and care-related supplies)

7. *The Caregiving Boom: Baby Boomer Women Giving Care,* National Alliance for Caregiving, September 1998, p. 8

8. "The National Nursing Home Survey: 1997 Summary", Table 25, p. 28, National Center for Health Statistics

9. Clark, Kim, "The New Midlife," *U.S. News & World Report*, March 20, 2000

10. *Projected Needs of the Aging Baby Boomers*, General Accounting Office, 6/91, GAO/HRD-91-86, p. 12 (Supported by Health Care Financing Administration's current projection of 5.8% for 1993-2008 in "The Next Decade of Health Spending: A New Outlook," *Health Affairs*, July/August 1999, p. 93)

11. Ibid.

12. "The National Nursing Home Survey: 1997 Summary", Table 1, p. 4, National Center for Health Statistics

13. "2000 Nursing Home Cost Survey" MetLife Mature Market Institute, Released July 24, 2000. (Nursing home costs include semi-private room rate plus an estimated 20% for miscellaneous charges, such as prescription drugs and care-related supplies)

Sources for Chapter 3:
Long-Term Care: The New Employee Benefit

1. Dychtwald, Ken, PhD, **AgePower**, Penguin Putnam, Inc. Publishers, 1999, p. 146

2. Ash, Patricia E., *U.S. Group Long-Term Care Insurance: 1999 Sales and In Force*, Life Insurance Market Research Association (LIMRA), 2000, and Coronel, Susan. *Long-Term Care Insurance in 1997-1998*, Health Insurance Association of America, March 2000

3. *Work-Family Roundtable—Juggling the Demands of Dependent Care*, The Conference Board, Winter 1997, p. 3

4. *Family Caregiving in the U.S., Findings from a National Survey*, National Alliance for Caregiving/AARP, 1997, p. 8

5. Ash, Patricia E., *U.S. Group Long-Term Care Insurance: 1999 Sales and In Force*, Life Insurance Market Research Association (LIMRA), 2000

6. "1999 Long-Term Care Survey," National Council on the Aging/John Hancock, p. 8

7. Dutton, Gail, "Benefits Soften Up," *HRfocus*, November 1998, p. 10

8. Pincus, Jeremy. *"Employer-Sponsored Long-Term Care Insurance: Best Practices for Increasing Sponsorship"*, Employee Benefit Research Institute Issue Brief 220, April 2000.

9. Pincus, Jeremy, "Employer-Sponsored Long-Term Care Insurance: Best Practices for Increasing Sponsorship," Employee Benefit Research Institute Issue Brief, April 2000, p. 9.

10. *USA Today, Weekend,* November 20-22, 1998

11. Galinsky, Ellen and Bond, James T., "The 1998 Business Work-Life Study: A Sourcebook," Families and Work Institute, p. 48

12. *Work and Elder Care: Facts for Caregivers and Their Employers,* U.S. Department of Labor, Women's Bureau, No. 98-1, May 1998, p. 3

13. Braus, Patricia, "When the HELPERS Need a Hand," *American Demographics,* September 1998, p. 69

14. "1999 Long-Term Care Survey," National Council on the Aging/John Hancock, p. 2

15. Coronel, Susan. *Long-Term Care Insurance in 1997–1998,* Health Insurance Association of America, March 2000, p. 26

16. *LTC Consultants* Semi-Annual Policy Comparison, January 2000

17. *Family Caregiving in the U.S., Findings from a National Study,* National Alliance for Caregiving/AARP, 1997 and "The MetLife Juggling Act Study: Balancing Caregiving with Work and the Costs Involved," Mature Market Institute, Metropolitan Life Insurance Company, November 1999, p. 2

18. Tilly, Jane, et al, **"Long-Term Care Chart Book: Persons Served, Payors, and Spending"**, The Urban Institute in Collaboration with the Congressional Research Service, May 5, 2000, p. 12

19. *Family Caregiving in the U.S., Findings from a National Study*, National Alliance for Caregiving/AARP, 1997, p. 33

20. *The MetLife Study of Employer Costs for Working Caregivers*, MetLife Mature Market Group, June, 1997, p. 3

21. Shellenbarger, Sue, "Work & Family: We Take Better Care of Our Elderly Parents Than Most Realize," *Wall St. Journal*, March 12, 1997

22. *Family Caregiving in the U.S., Findings from a National Study*, National Alliance for Caregiving/AARP, 1997, p. 12

23. *Ibid*

24. Schmidt, Jo Horne, "Who's Taking Care of Mom and Dad?" *Journal of the American Society of CLU & ChFC*, November, 1997, p. 83

25. *The MetLife Study of Employer Costs for Working Caregivers*, MetLife Mature Market Group, June, 1997, p. 18

26. "Elder Care and Death is an Avalanche Issue," *USA Today*, April 29, 1997, p. 2A

27. *National Family Caregivers Association/Fortis Final Report*, 1997

28. *USA Today, USA Snapshots*, June 16, 1997 (based on the National Council on Aging/John Hancock study)

29. "1999 Long-Term Care Survey," National Council on the Aging/John Hancock, p. 3

30. "The MetLife Juggling Act Study: Balancing Caregiving with Work and the Costs Involved," Mature Market Institute, Metropolitan Life Insurance Company, November 1999, p. 8

31. Doty, Pamela, Jackson, Mare E., and Crown, William, "Female Caregivers' Employment Status on Patterns of Formal and Informal Eldercare," *The Gerontologist*, June 1998, pp. 331-341

32. "1999 Long-Term Care Survey", National Council on the Aging/John Hancock, p. 3

33. *Family Caregiving in the U.S., Findings from a National Study*, National Alliance for Caregiving/AARP, 1997

34. Dychtwald, Ken, PhD, **AgePower**, Penguin Putnam, Inc. Publishers, 1999, p. 146

35. *The Breakthrough Intercessor*, an intercessory prayer ministry founded by Catherine Marshall, author of **Christy**, Lincoln, Virginia

36. *Family Caregiving in the U.S., Findings from a National Study*, National Alliance for Caregiving/AARP, 1997

37. *Who Buys Long-Term Care Insurance? 1994-1995 Profiles and Innovations in A Dynamic Market*, Health Insurance Association of America/Life Plans, Inc., pp. 18-19 (Confirmed with LifePlans, Inc., January 2001)

38. Tilly, Jane, *et al,* **"Long-Term Care Chart Book: Persons Served, Payors, and Spending,"** The Urban Institute in Collaboration with the Congressional Research Service, May 5, 2000, p. 12

39. *Facts and Trends*, "The Nursing Facility Sourcebook," American Health Care Association, 1999, p. 6

40. *Albany Times-Union*, March 8, 1998

41. Alligood, Leon, "Love Conquers All", *The Tennessean*, February 14, 1999, p. 1F

42. Chavez, Tim, "Their Love Story is One of Survival and Triumph," *The Tennessean*, February 13, 1999, p. 1B

43. Shelton, Phyllis R., President, *LTC Consultants*

44. Coronel, Susan. *Long-Term Care Insurance in 1997-1998*, Health Insurance Association of America, March 2000, p. 17

45. "Projected Need of the Aging Baby Boomers," General Accounting Office, 6/91, p. 12, GAO/HRD-91-86 (The Health Care Financing Administration also projects a similar average annual growth rate for 1993-2008 in "The Next Decade of Health Spending: A New Outlook," *Health Affairs*, July/August 1999, p. 93)

46. Rhoades, J.A and Krauss, N.A. "Nursing Home Trends, 1987 and 1996." Rockville (MD): Agency for Health Care Policy and Research, 1999, MEPS Chartbook No. 3, AHCRP Pub. No. 99-0032

47. *Ibid*

48. Bonde, Birgitta, Assistant to the Minister of Economic and Financial Affairs at the Swedish Embassy in Washington, D.C., February 2001

Sources for Chapter 4:
The Partnership for Long-Term Care

1. "2000 Nursing Home Cost Survey" and "2000 Home Health Care Cost Survey", MetLife Mature Market Institute, Released July 24, 2000.

2. Health Care Financing Administration, 1998 statistics

3. O'Brien, Ellen, Rowland, Diane and Keenan, Patricia. "Medicare and Medicaid for the Elderly and Disabled Poor," Kaiser Commission on Medicaid and the Uninsured, May 1999, p. 17

Sources for Chapter 5:
The Medicaid Benefit for Long-Term Care

1. Health Care Financing Administration, 1998 statistics

2. Shilling, Dana J.D. *Financial Planning for the Older Client*, 3rd edition, National Underwriter, 1997, p. 176

3. Margolis, Harry S., Esq,. *The ElderLaw Report*, Aspen Publishers, June 1998, p. 7 (*Golf v. New York State Department of Social Services*—CT. App. N.Y., Nov. 7, 1998 WL 151293, Apr. 2, 1998) and July/August 1998, p. 15 (*Chambers v. Ohio Department of Human Services*—U.S. Ct. App. 6th Cir., No. 96-3046, May 27, 1998)

4. Margolis, Harry S., Esq. "Purchase of Annuity Is Improper Asset Transfer", *The ElderLaw Report*, Aspen Publishers, May 2000, p. 7 *In re: Perkins* (Ohio Dept. of Human Services, Admin. App., Case No. 5040240805, Appeal Nos. 9932080 & 9936198, Docket No. 2000-AA-0085, Feb. 28, 2000)

5. Ibid. "N.D. High Court Rules State May Recover from Spouse's Estate," March, 1999, p. 5 (North Dakota Dept. of Human Services v. Thompson, N.D. Sup. Ct., Civil No. 980050, 1998 WI. 887673, Dec. 22, 1998)

6. Ibid. "Recipient's Assets Conveyed to Wife Are Recoverable from Her Estate," June 2000, pp. 5–6 (In the Matter of the Estate of Wirtz, N.D. Sup. Ct., No. 990275, 2000 WI, 291154, March 21, 2000)

7. Ibid. "HCFA Says Annuities May Be Recovered from Estates", March 1999, p. 5

8. Wilcox, Melynda Dovel. "Will Nursing-Home Bills Haunt Your Estate?" *Kiplinger's Personal Finance Magazine*, April 1998

9. O'Brien, Ellen, Rowland, Diane and Keenan, Patricia. "Medicare and Medicaid for the Elderly and Disabled Poor," Kaiser Commission on Medicaid and the Uninsured, May 1999, p. 17

10. *The Public Policy and Aging Report*, National Academy on an Aging Society, Summer 1999, p. 11

11. Graham, Ellen. "Work and Family: Should You Buy Insurance for Extended Elder Care?", *Wall Street Journal*, March 31, 1999, p. B1

12. Franklin, Mary Beth. "Knowing the Score," *Kiplinger's Personal Finance Magazine*, March 2000, p. 96

Sources for Chapter 6:
Alternatives for Financing Long-Term Care

1. "Accelerated Death Benefits, 1998," American Council of Life Insurance and LIMRA International, 1999, p. 7

2. Coronel, Susan, *Long-Term Care Insurance in 1997-1998*, Health Insurance Association of America, March 2000, p. 13

3. "Accelerated Death Benefits, 1998," American Council of Life Insurance and LIMRA International, 1999, p. 20

4. Case study provided by The Heritage Group, Oklahoma City, OK, a firm that specializes in life settlements

5. Chodes, Gary, "A Revolution in Higher-End Life Insurance," *Accounting Today*, November 8–21, 1999

6. Baskies, Jeffrey A. and Slafsky, Neal A., *Trusts & Estates*, June 1997

Sources for Appendix A:
Senior Benefits

1. Miller, Jessica, "The Changing Face of Long-Term Care", *CARING* Magazine, August 1998, p. 24

2. Dychtwald, Ken, PhD, **Healthy Aging: Challenges and Solutions,** Aspen Publishers, p. 210

3. "Out-of-Pocket Health Care Costs among Older Americans," *The Journals of Gerontology: Psychological and Social Sciences*, January 2000, Volume 55B, No. 1, p. S51

4. Ibid.

5. Mahkorn, Sandra, M.D., M.P.H., M.S., "How Not to Reform Medicare: Lessons from the Medicare+Choice Experiment," *The Heritage Foundation Backgrounder*, Publication No. 1319, September 15, 1999

6. "Out-of-Pocket Health Care Costs Among Older Americans," *The Journals of Gerontology: Psychological and Social Sciences*, January 2000, Volume 55B, No. 1, p. S52

ACKNOWLEDGMENTS

We gratefully acknowledge receiving help from the following publications and groups: *The 2000 Guide to Health Insurance for People with Medicare*, the **Long-Term Care Planning Guide**, 1999 Edition, The National Association of Insurance Commissioners, the State of Tennessee Department of Commerce and Insurance, and the following organizations and individuals who are there for you when you need them!

Health Care Financing
    Administration . . . . .Anna Long, Roger
                            Keene, Roy Trudel

U.S. Dept. of Health and Human
    Services National Center for
    Health Statistics . . . . Genevieve Strahan

The Agency for Health Care
    Research & Quality . . . . .Bill Spector, Ph.D.

Department of Health & Human
    Services Office of the Secretary for
    Planning & Evaluation . . . . .John Cutler

Bureau of the Census Population
    Division .Terry Lugaila

The Urban Institute . . . . .Brenda Spillman,
                                Ph.D.

Visiting Nurse Service of New York . . .Christopher M.
Murtaugh, Ph.D.

LifePlans, Inc. . . . . .Marc Cohen, Ph.D.,
Jessica Miller

Health Insurance Association of
America .Susan Coronel,
Matthew Binette

Life Insurance Market Research
Association (LIMRA) . . . . .Patricia Ash

The American Health Care
Association . . . . .Karen Mark

National Council on Aging . . . . .Mike Reinemer

National Association of Home Care . .Christina Robinson

Mr. Long-Term Care . . . . .Martin Bayne

Long-Term Care Group . . . . .Eileen Tell

National LTC Partnership Office . . . .Mark Meiners, Ph.D.

California Partnership for
Long-Term Care . . . . .Sandra Pierce-Miller

Connecticut Partnership for
Long-Term Care . . . . .David Guttchen, Mary
Pettigrew, Jim Palma

Illinois Partnership for
Long-Term Care . . . . .Jean Blaser

Indiana Partnership for
    Long-Term Care . . . . .Mary Ann Hack

New York State Partnership for
    Long-Term Care . . . . .Greg Belardi

Brandeis University . . . . .Christine Bishop,
                                            Ph.D.

Osborne & Associates . . . . .Tim Osborne, CPA

Tennessee Department of Insurance . . .Howard McGill

Kansas Department of Insurance . . . . .Tom Foley

Centennial Adult Care Center . . . . . .Stephen Zagorski

Center for Long-Term Care
    Financing . . . . .Steve Moses

Elder Law Attorney . . . . .Harry Margolis, Esq.

Elder Law Attorney . . . . .Dana Shilling, J.D.

Elder Law Attorney . . . . .Timothy Takacs, Esq.

Trust Attorney . . . . .Al Secor, J.D.

Alabama Medicaid . . . . .Michelle Urban

Florida Medicaid . . . . .Lynn Raichelson,
                                            Debbie Peterson

Georgia Medicaid . . . . .Alan Hill,
                                            Sharon Damsgward

New York Medicaid . . . . .Barbara Barnes,
                                            Betty Rice

CNA . . . . .Dick Garner

John Hancock/Fortis . . . . .Mike Steinhardt

Golden Rule . . . . .Scott Berghuis

John Hancock . . . . .Glenda Copeland

MetLife .Joyce Ruddock,
                                           Holly Dantuono

Nationwide . . . . .Tom Houle

Prudential . . . . .Gail Holubinka,
                                           Nancy McGee

The Travelers . . . . .Kyle Rothery

UNUM . . . . .Peggy Murray

The Heritage Group . . . . .Tom Moran

LTC Consultants
   National Trainers . . . . .Catherine Dove,
                                           John Ferroni,
                                           David Miller, CLTC
                                         and Randy Smith

Financial Freedom . . . . .Paulette Wisch

MedStat . . . . .Brian Burwell

Association of Health
   Insurance Advisors . . . . .Diane Boyle

and the wonderful staff of LTC Consultants without which
nothing would ever be printed!